These names whose
power is expressed by
the first letter of the
word.

the Characters.

anger   ore

around   virgin

it   error

ire   ache

odds   church

HARRIOT
DOUBLE

HARIOT DOUBLE

Gavin Selerie

with graphics
by Alan Halsey

FIVE SEASONS PRESS · 2016

Published June 2016 by
Five Seasons Press
41 Green Street
Hereford HR1 2QH, UK

www.fiveseasonspress.com
books@fiveseasonspress.com

ISBN 978-0-947960-89-6

Gavin Selerie's design
typeset in Ehrhardt
at Five Seasons Press
and printed on
Five Seasons recycled paper
by Short Run Press UK

FRONT COVER:
Image by Alan Halsey

BACK COVER:
Photographs of author
by Andrew Bullett (magnum)
and Frances Presley (statue)

joe harriott
'i've filed it under question mark'

Tom Raworth, *Catacoustics*

I kept on, with Hariot fading in and fading out

Muriel Rukeyser, *The Traces of Thomas Hariot*

Contents

INTERMEAN

TWO

Prologue

after Muriel Rukeyser

What are the three sea marriages?
Were the metal soldiers cast as a game?
What castle is on Sleep Hill?
What is a dot?
How many infinities?
How do you get from a prison to the Moon?
What is the horse half–leaping out of the world?

I

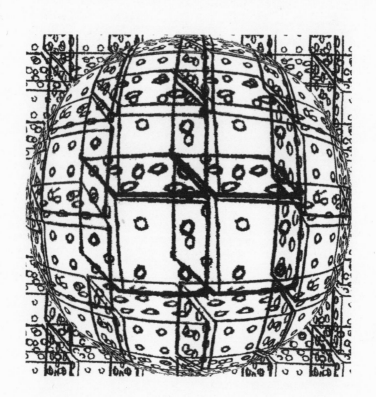

Formation

Heard the ward an orphan go
Joe Arthurlin Jizmun
out of cane and indigo towers
for muse-ache bent
he's grained to discover
now sister Ignatius
say you can blow xaymaca
summit or sonnet
a cheek tale, akee all split.

As if from nothing
a seed a stalk
reaches.

Alpha boy
mammee-sapota, grenadilla
from a devotion bell
geds hard travail
to play off d'frame.

Kingston, Surrey
nuff nuff rememba drops
this wul' shall shift
a snaky orchid
sniff to tell
how dreams come back
still the rain beat
tap tap tap
on a zinc roof.

Mi a forward, foot
in a piece of rosy pink
enlarged from map—
no medz without the trouble.

Linstead Flash

Hauled over Bog Walk
can see the river still, cobra crawlin lazy
till it put on a brown suit
and roll.

Egret is there on bamboo-legs,
stoops to catch a fish. Dey all
figure, will fly to a branch
or stack of rock.

July sun, no father come,
he's playing green and lucky.

If you ain't start, don't learn that game—
should be atop, with frangipani scent.

*****

What's left the mother do
but under de railings
lay out sum fruit, laugh a dole-song:

Carry me ackee, go a–market
five chains down the road,
not a quatee wud sell,
lawd wat a night, not a bite.

Black seed on butter, you want some
body gorge. Sweet cries
through a wrap, bell at 5 am
or dangling ring in a glass.

X-pression again: push that photo
beneath de mattress, it's not true
you win you gotta be bad.

*****

Scrawl in chunks of mud, an odda
replaces no saint. Why'n't you bring
a whistle or a bag of marbles?

Here's a pick-cha book,
put yo'self on de cover:
blue glaze sky, ripe breadfruit
to mek a fambly swell.

Dat cost dear with a line of crosses.

Fahwud shake down blood corridor,
face of beginning joy.

Death will strut in de carnival glare,
come in your house
as a babe dun open its mouth.

Fever up whitewash walls.

She's gone to ghost-land,
went without tellin'. The door is closed,
just sleep outside till morning.

Six years out the toys whisper:
whose boy is you?

Vector

Down between white tablets
sheer to the sky. *Tightly hold
her hand. Know this
and you don't.* A winding thread
with green flanks—
maidenhair, trees stacked
top out of root.

More to be learnt, hemmed
below Pum Pum Rock,
her socks and veil. Swing across
Flat Bridge, a startled lizard
by crazy silver.

Angels, old sugar-land,
then Spanish Town, sleepy saints
parade. *O lackadaddy,
time for a bite or jink.*

Last scuttle-track—*carts out
of de way*—into Kingston.
Tramcars, people stuck like flies,
ricky-tick, balang-bang,
a dilly-dally bundle-grip
'bout big stores.

Victoria Park, Queen Street,
deh deh, a flagged empire
up to Mercy gates
dust can't medghure.

Shake out today, must jump up
a little Man.

Alcove Arms

You don't go to school all day,
you do music de other half. To hold a horn
you got to be better than two or three people.
Little chance you get, you do as much as you can.

It's a bag to something jammy
and you don't harch off. Sisters has a story
for all you do. Come out the monkey puzzle,
what will your mudda do if you stay
and don't come down. It says in the book
a grime boy will return. By narrow lanes
to a pockmarked wall.

Iggy show the gold is in learning,
there's no badmind catch. Madonna,
she hold our life in glass, a line ov figures
set for somewhere else. Dey turn
from an iron bed, dusty shutters
to blue mountains and breeze.
Why oughtn't—South Camp Road
spangles in solution.

De phrase you make, glancing off,
was took a lap ago, same town about
cross de sea.

Cane to Cube

Just another day
you understand,
jus' normal folks.
If we don't talk
the same it's still
to us the Kane's
English. We don'
tell the time by
no hand sticking
around the clock
face, just watch
de sun: when he
comes up over
the tree-top we
jus gets going in
to the canefield.
This Monymusk
estate sure has
a lot of cane. The
company won't
stan for no trash.
You has to cut
off the top and
take the trash off
the side. O, that
don't worry me
overmuch, cause
I've been cutting
cane since I was
knee high to an
alligator. Then
there's loaders
stack the wagon
goes to de fact'ry
mighty hungry
to cut and roll so
the boat can fill.

London dockside: raw sugar in
sacks. Impure crystals brown &
sticky with molasses. You drain
off the treacle to get to a lighter
colour, pump: spiked arms over
a strainer, liquid gas, a pressure
filter, coil of pipes. A pan makes
40 tons in 2 hrs. Cascade damp
through warm air or pour hot to
mould for setting hard in slabs
which, dry, are cut into CUBES
all clean & white—empire tight.

Gripsack

Sunny skies don't harmonize,
de can's empty, it's a Monday kind
of Friday.

> *Jamaica don't you muck-rake her,*
> *she got sea grapes and calabash,*
> *all tings to feed de spirit.*

They build me up, fingers and lips
to do an out-chorus.

> *Scrape to make a shack shack,*
> *rattle a beat for home.*

Rise everyday, pelican on de palisadoes,
must let myself a-loose.

> *Debble passport slides you down.*

Smoke in de breeze, steamship
gwine to take her.

> *Gangway to where, you tink.*

King's head on a penny—
what's on de odder side?

> *Flip and a shield divides the date.*

One arms is a kind of promise
island to island, turbine
veins probing. I'll know a place
I never was.

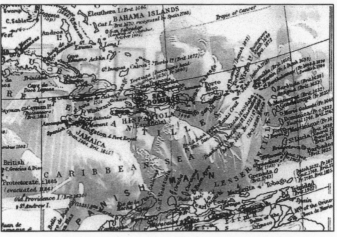

Trance Port

Ship out on a liner
turn again Geraldo
through tinsel seaweed

to Cork, Southampton
grey oily rollers, grey sun
over endless quay, track and switches.

Prospect pukka, out of the pen
or vale royal, blue classical avenue,
that's de place, all well come
to mother crease
it do promise
the ol' pride and grace.

Blacked out, no paint, aftermath rations
the heart is a cellar
with pulse steps
on a diamond pavement.

Late off the job these natives is hungry
for alto, injecting chat
like smokepole stabs
to find the moon in Wardour Street.

Can I fluent Caliban
get accust, a–costumed
to this colony of tunnellers
whose blinking
bounce and beckon
makes phospho Babylon
the place to be.

Uncap the bottle in Rik's grot,
blow a riff, righteous sweet
into alcoves sweated
with perfume, powder,
a boat hold of honour
and slithery silk.

▷

Is it a radiator squeals
all poses by appointment
that arch says
impro over order
mewses must exist.

Suave Silvius beneath tatty daub
hears walla walla walla (don't bat
an eyelid)
holiday OK but don't stay.

Brave Kingdom

Got it all like letters on de telephone dial,
not just a number to find a name.
There's chi-chi bud in grey-gold streets,
jewelled skies from Holborn to Marble Arch.

Lipso-lanto, slip through Time
dat's a rollick box or stiller ring.

Big Ben, Abbey and Tower, dey bounce up
3-D, more than a toy at de fair.
People going nowhere, just in a hurry,
red-brick faces over beaming profit.

Every new dress, can't help but follow,
pearl of a strutter with leisure rubbed in.
Every new talk mek a telegraph wire, O lord
this lan' is a jangle of surprises.

Got it all, pound of kiss, four inch of tongue,
a basinful to live. Glass doors and lift
to a treasure sack, den down by a fountain
wid winged paradighty spirit.

Selvedge

Talk of colour/absent mark
against identity. Only
what has been.

Tall houses stuck together,
soggy grass.

This is the clay, the water for me.

Two-tone code, shirt and suit,
if you want to fit.

A garden square locked tight,
railings over the cellar.

Crystal mannequin heads
that cry out and vanish.

With nothing to do
you can feel a millionaire.

Give the arrangement another shake
or accent the wrong syllable,
a shell survives.

In Alpha I got grounation,
a mouth to speak.

I spy, I try.

Tonal

Plum talk is just the way we got it
out there. More Britt-ysh in pitch
than the clipped drawl that toggles
here. My bell is not the zipzap
thing, it comes like the moon
through a window, gold filigree
on the wall. I can say *hapstickle*
but that's toddy from another tree.
I knew this game before I saw it—
club-wise stride in silver tie
with red stripe. You can't be just
an equal. Beneath one pediment
I'd draw half the world, chops
outworking any catalogue of habit.

Indents

No need to stand around
in Archer Street

where thumbs are half
(meaning ten Bob)

    What can chance
    beyond spaffled chat

    comes parallax

this you there you
shall be

    billed on boards

face in a bottle-green sea
stencil name

    over white sheet

idol bleed
out of
just business

    adept in dicey premises
    the record
    speaks

Got a wave through
today

Booster

Walk anywhere (by demand)   door after door
    clamber steps   in star-daze

       Afro-Cubist   *Cottontail*—
        that can't   be it

         smile with Monk
           in Paris

          fast echo
        (blows belief)
     Albert Hall

    Ronnie's Big Band—Samson & Hercules (N'wch)
      to Morecambe stand-fight

Third place in poll   nearly a horse ahead

Dulcephone mecca platters   gold on blue
triangle push-out centre   less crackle and hiss

        No sorcery
       just science

      air sucked in
       let out

That's funny   this watch has five hands
   did I   stakely bring

     beams   through filtered lace

Poppet Stretch

Sohoe, the hare ys founde

A cup of news on Froth Street, Gaggia-drawn
like a glimpse of first television

       Cupid's bubble
    off two-tone formica

dream in spoonful sips a line of suitors

       beribboned
      between Windmill
    & St Giles's Field

where present sense is the sheen

      from matchable
    shadows

Love-toys and philo-freaks
charmly bruited

      tea-cake
    or banana split

man-watch without saying

      you *can* smile after all,
    nice little figure, well stacked

nothing but top of the milk

Late Spot

Try him.
There's still a while to go.
How many others?
Forget the arithmetic.
Till April dear. Too clever
if you ask me. Nice little tale
for a quiet party. You wouldn't
want to lose the chance. I've had
a bit of practice. Not shy then?
Over there. Not from that angle.
I haven't got one on at all.
Don't tell anybody though. What's that?
We haven't got any petticoats on.
You lovely things. Don't let it
become a habit. Anyone special?
We don't trust cockney.
You stopping the night then?
Why? Think I'm not flush enough
to use a taxi? Got any Scotch?
Ooh they're pairing off. Oo-rh, hey girl.
I don't know whether I can take this.
Out of fairness you know—I'll share.
Yeah man, go boy. I love this.
Oh don't go darling.
Joseph, I wish you were
sitting somewhere else, love
cause I don't like to be . . .
Turn it round, a bit of blues.
Something with a bit of—thingy, soul.
Isn't it romantic—ba-ba-ba, sha-la-la.
OK—a-one-two-three-four . . .

Black on White

Snow–smile   blue eyes
    honey–curve   hair

         off–limit
         scent

            from
          far suburbs

      firm shoulder
     fixed stare

   Soho   lilting
suit   command

Areola

You must be older than *that*

a giggle to dare

sky deep gaze,
vanilla cheek

Wriggles out of
a flame-ribbed jersey

faster breath

twin-rings, risen

clasp and let go

Kinsey Rite

Press

that　　gold

button　　　　now the

planet　　　　　swivels

that's how　　　　　it starts

a number　　　　　　ash-kept

crooning　　　　　　rekindles

alphabet　　　　　　offsplay

through　　　　　　narrow

drink in　　　　　　passage

to flock　　　　　　quarter

for your　　　　　　decca'd

five-sum　　　　　wingbeat

as flamingo in railway arms

the cell–estial call sign

Compound

Who killed the carpenter?—
panting stakes and bicycle chains.

Away from the whole shoot,
bag wash laundry stuff,
blobber-lips at empire ruin,
now can I count twelve rocking
or trace it out in Pinewood suite.

Quiet trees off the Devil's Highway,
white-walled ward in south-facing arc.
Aboard a bed, might be at sea,
it's not too late. Salt, pearls
sparkle. A nurse carries the dish
to bring on sleep. Where is
that lyric? Lull the clatter
of your beating ear. No fag
for once lodged in sassophone.

Darling on a page of wishes,
is—ever—of some moment sketched,
playroom to the right elbow
interlaced with cordage. Cootchie
chest. Speak, speak.

Fish scales on half-lit water. A shroud
flaps gently. Ideas wriggle
to salve a rotten ladder.
Calico takes the rougher print.

Backward to engine thrum
the radio's stuck with old prevailers.

There might be another way:
toss and crevulate, the Ching
answers.

▷

Lattice marks on tilted ceiling,
spiky reach
of puppet hand

▬▬▬▬▬ floor
▬▬▬▬▬ mind
▬▬ ▬▬ sky

trigrammatic

the subject
bubbles up

Treatment

A chart with cartoon lines added
begins to climb the wall

      temperature   dashes
         up
             and
   down

strange as Linear B   (might as well cry
            for the moon)

not exactly a death cell but—
what's that shadow on your breather
apparatus?

       10 am
       brisk from habit
       Dr Poles will do her rounds

'how are you today, *Harriott?*'
(army style)

       pluck a little reduced,
       sleepy smile

Light oddly cubic   bears
           a slash and curve

big manuscript sheet, propped on knees

   blow—press—pull—tap

   neither lead nor backup

Parish Without

Scent of pine needles on dry soil,
better than a voyage to Egypt.

Sticks cast out, speaking
more laws than you know.

Belt of trees against wind and rain,
air free to turn.

Forget any clock-tread, breathe
ahead and back

leaf-oil to blood current
in a burdened chest

green finding red
down wracked tubes

equal as a thing you might
invent, off beyond right here

Subcore Frisk

---

moon/moonwort fern| |BELL ◉ heather
dwarf gorse

---

pine ARROW
midheart midheart| |sprote Δ sheer

Bagshot   awash then boney–dry   stock jobbed
   sand   Tudor smother

---

flit flut rout agog ago   wish–tery   ramping royal
flugel   wakes   on   Nine Mile Ride   to chelp

---

  dim rim tip   der   da   der   da
dug run tug   PLY   der   dum   der   dum

Pinewood to Paddington

Back to what lusorious lots
dis-turb *zenfolia*: dose of Glenfiddich
to roll the jackpot,
nurse in a silk blouse dancing
before chipped marble.

You put out your hands in mime—
can manage a bit of solo piano,
Body and Soul, but the horn is waiting
for breath.

Don't know where the dark dark
dominus drives. See lamps
down a steel blade road
where beetles slide.

Maybe music will come
from skipped meals, as from a suitcase
a bird sings. It has to be different
this December, now green eyes blink
in oil and rust.

Around this cube curtains cling
like winter feathers. Pieces of furniture
squeak to undrudge the clock.
A forest swells in a closed off alley.

Loxodrome

Plot the pattern, leave blanks for what
you don't know

                    smoke, wind
             over tropic line

                            on bulbous box

                a body stretch
             at star-cross

all turning strait   by rum
                      or *room*

lodestone peak   maybe

        so stare   (steer)
by hung sheets   tomorrow

Court Sunday

In from Henglish drizzle, before was pale sun, we got
reverse faith. Only compellance is free pints
to toast a new arrival. Slide mongoose, yu name
bounce up with pasparall. Fight yuh way to the back
and feel it good time, not please-sir-in' a future
lick of salt. Smell how fe have respect roun' this
balm-yard—you look me look, cross timbales.
Tempo hottin' anyone can join, keys or whatever
on a bottle. All a de elements does mek
meander, sharp. No boogu yagga lie dung here,
it's tryout till yuh wilt, best heffort at ketching a'fire.
Come leh we parang, pictures on the walls, ash trays
does be in tune. Strange face is no debar, tight smile
find easy drawl. Handshake, how's your glass,
step in 'nother shoe. Bunch of tings, some yuh know,
seed like Players. When one is out, another one in.

Flexy

Say something, anything
but in your accent.

Don't know what to say,
the monkey won't do.

Give us a picture of home.

Higgler squattin on de curb,
give me canned sausage, matches.

Sounds exotic.

The boat me come from has memory fits.
Flogged out, the pain do count.

Sure there's nothing I can do?

You can lime with me at the lime tonight,
find riddim—wind like crazy.

Dangerous, is it?

Green guava down dere, yuh mouth explodes
in spurts of sour.

So, is this the real you?

A triangle in a box makes the colours come.
Let's get back to here.

M★★Q★★★ Recall

Down past a carousel horse to the basement
sprung beneath film

Tilted stripe roof, wall-cogs, pillars
wrapped with carpet

a big oval

LADIES AND GENTLEMAN—
TONIGHT THERE ARE . . .
584 OF US IN HERE

packed curve

tricky passage pondered, spray if you get
too close

nine-piece
reach
with   bongos
congas   space
to solo
and share

tint of crushed pine-cone
knife below shoulder blade

jubilant
blues
to
mark release

out through the back
to the Coach & Horses, spin out
a scotch with Ginger ale

Troy-game

The Chube, a single dancing path
to the heart

tells in glass
some tale suspended

bassa–bassa, take me out—
it's too damn fine and not enough

arms of green leather, seat
a diamond moquette

straphanger bobbles
averted gaze

***

That west end call, the colony spot
might be a life

mokha, raddled girder,
sweat-stained walls

press, pinion your tongue
to find—*gr, guh*—and twine

beast, beauty, as a roll
through   hollow wind

***

Perplexed in the round
we get there straight

World in a Kiss

It's better if the last scene
comes first, do me that turn
the sextant of sex
so cried up

can you see
a rhom–rhom boidal
rhythm of stars

glow–points
in a net

glass beads, scribbles
on a beach

lurchy *dip-dop*
laughter–waves
under screen of silence

we touch crumblejumble

whirling sky–signs, mammoth traffic—
ever–ready lashes, our soul Circus

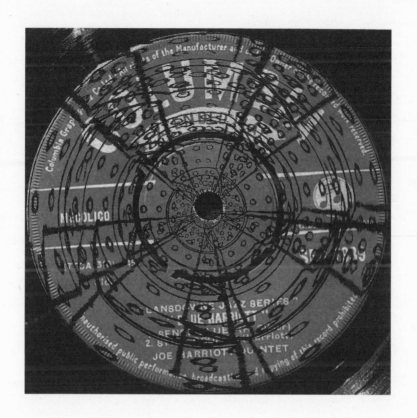

Fishin' the Blues / You'll Never Know

Big black eagle, sharp suit, trim beard,
one side close
draws a probing gaze.

    That whole history in a solo
    falls from a knot,
    grip-route
    out of fulgurous jolts
    frantic, easy
    to the pitch and take-up.

A trayful of drinks in drifting smoke.
What converts to a human face?

Propped at the bar, after-hours
in squelchy limbo
she craves some special julep

takes him home, has to check
her husband's out,
wants to be whipped over a piano.

Corners, we meet in
corners, can't play
that hanging-in, the tune
just don't allow. Can't keep
when another's coming.

Skulliban shrugs, don't worry
love's a scamel, filbert, marmoset
plucked from a crevice.

You lick a shifting tide, by limb splay
look to jump the wreck, beam-float,
laugh as the loss goes good. Bury all
with a chorus.

Pictures drop from a white mouthpiece
till sassafras winds to Clifton Hill,
twelve foot by ten—a nutshell safe—
and half at least alone.

A ballad is the heart
behind the hard, algebra
of stifled need.

Deccalian

A still box
with ribbed front

smooth steel arm
over sprung table

click, gentle buzz

pull to the right and start

drop, crackle,
furrow to centre

vertigo runes

then deft dial
through field

echoes
of bird
in flight

Micro-drift

rock

pool

splash   screech
                          from
roundel   murmur
                          at
to   brink

compass

Silent Key

Is it a dream or remembered text, the shift
this afternoon

a breeze through the room, a bright light
all around

veins in the wall, carpet, ceiling-work

this place a white glow, the cloud right down
to the kerbstones

as a verse in the heart, a sense planted—
all has a point

Tate Picks

As I think them, not as I see them
the head goes into two or three.
A mask turns, this what
comes strangely—skin, bone
in tidal geometry.

You see through the blood
in cloth, hold a fleeting
solid. She's a hatched leaf
in back breeze, house or country
cut against soil.

From room to room the frames
unremembered
make a slopey world
not gilt, silk or marble. A stain
on floor polish is a million feet
from Silvertown.

Tear, twist, jam. A knotted nerve
splay. Web stares.

One who you might follow
to lead is a simply complicated
thing: just the *look of* means.

His book at the fifth stage goes—
to be there is not *there*. Space builds
in the box that's more outside.
A flat break who scans it
nitches another.

Millbank: July/Sept. 1960

Quex-aught

To paint smoke   it's got to be so
you can drive a nail   through it

        an ear lobe
        clasped hands

the stuff   you'd latch

      then let it ga-ga-go
      and start

Alogism

Spanglish

r
i
v
e
n

SAZO   FAUN

Soundbrush

Verem
lovYing

foregates
awlle
liemight

onder   moans of moans on calumns

dat plie a perfarmer non saleep

wid imnet swailscud

Vieshuns a zoumbai wad fload

spone und sizars fram hellsware

yanO ets da killenghaast

Tongdrooth

6I   suchlaik   wungoze

bekauz   dobell

by grogged raysum
on mopamound

racerider in chimesmoke   Jaw

sheeny slotbox idol   Hare

Moquedd   niled prop   eye add

seed

Queen

red   Tate

buzz   nexties   forst

$U1^e$

vy vom
vum   jus
scope id owd

Roost

Life behind stucco

just one photo (of Charlie Parker)

a record–player, Parker records,
some Sonny Stitt

Rice and peas
on the stove

rare piece of mango

Next door on the upright:

this is how a Trinidadian
would play it
and here's the Jamaican way

Which is the most difficult?

shift a mountain with a teaspoon,
drain an ocean cup by cup
or borrow £5 from the barman

Tommy Atkins portage to the next frame

Grid Switch

```
MEKMITELYUHWEAREDDIGOTDIMEENSFIPROBE
S                                   F
E                                   O
M                 C                 R
O             A        I            E
K          N              O         S
E        B              S           T
F          E        G    T          L
I                 E                 Y
S                                   S
L                                   H
A                                   A
N                                   N
T                                   G
P                                   O
E            effyamindwhats         D
E            slowedaprism           A
P            itfleksanoda           T
R            bashment               K
D            boddle                 Y
R            Base                   A
I            uv                     N
V                                   G
E                                   L
Z                                   E
STEWJOEWHEELSFSAINTDENISMIDCUBICWOMB
```

Cowbell and Tumbler

Brought the good news
that's what I want to do, paint pictures
so whatever you hear is there.

Gawky Flamingo, just goofin'
at the stokehole
all night spotlit airless
in sea–spit cavern.

Brown sounds from a few short notes
the musial circuit
steals
to deliver.

D–difficult racket, caw from ruin
to Lansdowne leafy block
its staircase winding
to basement den.

House of Shattering Glass:
walls chimneys upward speak
through back–number flesh
a cluster of names—
Ricketts & Shannon, Robinson and Pryde
down to Forbes & Philpot
the craft instilled, bloodway cut.

Go roundabout this, I'll play and you overshadow.

Shake and Cole,
you play this (spare) to start
and see what (ridge)
happens.

Allapse of tales,
pocket of remembrance sprung
in a murmur of brushes.

Soar and tumble, zigzag
across a jaunty dance
with bleary howls.

Coated folding ephemerid
sprite
breaks mel-odic

rule by least
a–goad
the dimdown old heartscape.

All the others they play here in d'room
but what I play is out d'window.

Out stuff we bounce off
(the wrong is just the passing)
till three numbers in
we're swallows on the water.

You're only as good as your next (not your last).
Sunset hush to Vesuvian night
to bird bird morning.

Neverworn no imitation,
the habit's local (Lonedom) made.

All this talk of over dare, Parker's scent—
it's not the place, it's you.

Tap out the notes of body and soul,
unscrew the inscrutable.

Rolling Log

January

21st: Royal Festival Hall, London (mat)
21st: Dome, Brighton (eve)
22nd: Victoria Palace, London
23rd: Town Hall, Birmingham
24th: De Montfort Hall, Leicester
25th: Colston Hall, Bristol
26th: Philharmonic Hall, Liverpool
27th: Free Trade Hall, Manchester
28th: Odeon, Leeds
29th: Gaumont, Hammersmith

April

9th: Hotel Leofric, Coventry
10th: Mermaid Hotel, Birmingham
11th: Fighting Cocks, Wolverhampton
12th: Crown & Anchor, Longton
13th: The Cavern, Liverpool
14th: White Eagle Club, Nottingham
15th: The Winking Skull, Oldham
16th: Down Beat Club, Newcastle
17th: Maryland/Amphora, Glasgow
18th: Tempo (Sporranslitters) Club, Edinburgh

Stop the car, I want to sleep

Inseam

Aug 24th—Paris Theatre,
free form for BBC. Given stopwatch
to count down to the red
or green light ('On Air'). Petrified
I would miss the second for transmission.
Lord Montague had a long talk with Joe
afterwards. Very keen.
Aug 26th—Richmond,
blazing sun, almost got stung
by a wasp. They came on
between Don Rendell & Tubby Hayes—
risked some 'out' stuff. Trad types
sat open-mouthed. Then
to the Marquee and an all-nighter
at Rik Gunnell's. Both blitzed,
good thing it was a weekend.
Sept 13th—Ronnie's, pretty full.
Joe played standards, I didn't know
what time it was, Loverman, What's New.
Some abstract, not sure which,
liquid across the room.
Audience stayed quiet for one solo,
magic. Then a murderously fast blues.
Sept 21st—Joe working Satire Club.
He had £1 from me.
25th—Joe had £1 from me.
Did not come home.
26th—Joe had a £1 from me.
Poured the contents of his pockets
on the chest of drawers.
Oct 30th—Met Joe at the Cottage Club.
He had £5 from me. Still four packs
of Senior Service a day, taxis
and fruit machines.
31st—Argument. Went out, locked me
in the house.
Nov 5th—Still love him. Felt a little dizzy.
Left with what I brought, plus
little glass Bambi.

▷

Took flat in Kilburn, with Sue,
just up the road.
Nov 23rd—Went to collect some things.
Said I couldn't go back. He cried.
Bedroom fireplace painted over
in bright colours, bars of music
on a canvas in the living room. Picasso
again. Asked me what I thought.
Their session (day before) was 'like that'.
Dec 4th—Saw him at Ronnie's.
Went back. He hit me (first time),
broke down in tears (couldn't believe
he'd done it). Said it was like a record
come out wrong.
Dec 5th—Joe called me at work.
Wanted to meet. Said No.
He came to Kilburn with chocolates.
Sweetie, darlin', monkey face.
We'll start the New Year new.
Jan 2nd—Can't let go and can't go on.
Feb. Spoke on phone twice,
went to 94a. Merrydown
at the Clifton. All charming,
some laughs and the match routine
(one hand). Old fondles and such.
He asked about the check-ups.
April 28th—Zachary born.
October. If I go back
nothing will change.

Shred Rank

Pictures spelling out, how free is free? If abstract
who composed it, a theme that lets you bleat away
like sheep squelching through a quagmire
in a hail storm. What your regular gets at the table
is a tortured drum roll over a bass rumble of pleasure.
The number goes kim-kam, if one was ever born
where nothing swings. You need to be light as a bird
not a feather. Money down, expect the goods—
you can pick up glass eyes in Portobello Road.
Can structures lack structure? Is the sax a piece
of twisted metal, is the piano a rubber wedge?
Say you're talking—past a sub-standard mass—
why not play in the wings, perhaps in pyjamas?

[*Muse Rag Bites*]

CLUB diary

this is supposed to be objective thinking. Plymouth was a desert but Joe Harriott spent a few days varying the speed of the air column. You must soar. not in the least worried about Free Expression to a certain place in the TAPE ROOM. Fast, complicated, difficult like the sound from a battlefield at Mr. Ronnie Scott's hamburger heaven licensed bar open three till eleven. "We set a slowish tempo and everybody blew" a nightingale-in-a-scented-garden dockyard effect with probing fog horns & brassy clank of train couplings clattering like watching a film in which the dialogue is all in Swahili one hardly knew whether to award a "U" certificate or an "X" harmonically hung up on a chord more than most "evergreen sx" in flat keys that found their way between the Devil and the BBC into the most open of all A minor. Personal appearance often described Ornette Coleman with a local dance band real jazz played by real jazzmen imminent danger of Down Home Rag Coventry Birmingham Wolverhampton Longton Oldham a special apppearance at the Cavern

THE GO-ANYWHERE PLAY-ANYTIME

SAXOPHONES

Sop. Borgani brand new, lacquered with case	£95
Alto Selmer Mk VI..	£110
Alto Selmer Cigar Cutter..	£85
Alto Conn late model	£100
Alto Selmer S.A. ..	£90
Alto Selmer Bal' Action ..	£85
Alto Martin	£75
Tenor Selmer Radio-Imp. as new	£125
Tenor Selmer Mk VI recon.	£150
Tenor Buffet reconditioned	£110
Tenor Martin excellent ..	£60
Tenor Selmer Pennsylvania	£55
Tenor Borgani	£100

MINIVOX 'C'
Runs on batteries—Sounds like a mains set
41 ans.

the fanatics shouting for a bongo feature Dankworth Harriott Lightfoot Ball The British think there's something wrong with staying out all night the Tempos were the highest we'll get on Trad Tavern for a while

Juncture

A goblet with liquid flashing. Trickle of words,
a message here and gone. The last Trump,
bronze over granite, some film-fix. Whirr of giant
insects, a doll string in hectic passage. What's
it all for, this pageant disgorged, gamingly
sharp with a stoat's eye. Can't sit still,
stand still or lie still. Gauzes and silks glide above
with underworld steps, crimson, green, violet.
The last scrap at the centre, a distorted triangle,
could offer help, winged and graceful
but his basin is dry as fingers point
to cracks of a grimy pavement. It will not die,
your paradise in stone or metal. To cry
one syllable as *fire* or *out* may hold it whole,
meeked from dreams of having
the perfect surface. Away from blatting and blaring
you find better ground, glass melted to suggest a map.
Maybe it's a state not a place: as near down as up
and up as down, behind as before,
before as behind, on one side as other.
Hidden sound with the force of breath, hint
of text through an interleaf, strand of hair felt again
on the cheek. Beauty slows in a shafted circle
after gossip, the sky beckons, won't be done
for a shilling. No orders on a gridded dial, no juror
to bind this striate form. A player with a hollow
body makes a little plot reach far, pivots
on joy, his foreign dart thrown naked at dawn.

Jazz Moon

Once in a mist—east of—how high
she totters, her gauzy slink
one proud polka dot (oh beg yr pardon)
over a lo'down floor

      dream-rondel, felted
      spirit, her cleft and mound
      show up in fuzzy script

rays explosive, smooth shores
speak each record across bulbant time

      bucket or boat marks
      for a Maida hero
      just off Watling Street

black flint on red gravel—
flung far and hugged close
a north-west streak
through sleepy villa slopes,
plate glass parades,
tremble-rap factories and fields

      to reach those waves
      in flaming glass
      reared (there's my label)

she's my, she's my
smoky angel
grey-blue eyes, golden cheeks
shines her light on me

      forrid down to toecaps,
      nerves and marrow

saxogleam or cymbal shimmer,
copper to starry brass,
harks back a curl of hair,
scented neck

how Lucia glides magnetic
    above
a grubby papered cell

O-val throb, awake in sleep
she's a phrase knocking at the window
of syllabic graft, no ghost-face
but licorously present
to stir what's trapped in stone

    as if for the first, always
    a mix of trust and surprise

lashtender gets you thinking
in extended space
is this
breathable air, drumhead
to tone hole on Brute island's
squeezed frame, twin of giddy Lamp-town

3 and 4 in 7, horney and moist
at night's noon
what's sent a trifle becomes a treasure

that truth drops
from the sky

    a snow-owl
    perched
    on upended stake or pencil tower

    mistletoe-eyes
    over broken arch, drain and hellebores

you clutch, spark out of rubble
a prism pure in dust

    drawing the cry
    from a spun table

sapphire on wax

Rose Dawn

Most out of the world
you're with it

      conjur man, tinct me

dipped cloudy at sea
smoked in vault or tower

go wail between keys
a creature of herbs and gum

a flame in a crystal globe
ever-burning
crimson, green to blue

play the feel of the rose inside
dewy furls

crux-cup
      bone-bower
melding carol

roll in world-wreath what's
fluke found, all at once
brimmed a sum of years, a spirit
to hold

it's just there
in the porch tiles
the wallpaper
the fireplace

orb to square, she's at the seam
of this island home
a bed to remember some

ribanded consort,
scrolled night-cushion,
engraffed cabinet, so jantill
still after noise

see what's wiped
re-as-semble
the moon take one
belly and back

a regular day maybe walkin'
for summady gives the push, is where
you been—votch-arooni—
stretches the game
to be true

    one step luminous
        from nigredo stairs

the mantel scanning, stone above iron

      a damp reed from
    a giddy buffet

inverted 'J',
tarnished golden vessel

slumps in . . . a personal message,
'S' for shroud-eye

Don't worry, Joe (say it again)
they can't trace this snake letter,
can't cancel your name

Angelhorn

One about is really wannem out—
red botch (rid you)

You don' have to like me

gooseneck, bow, bell,
spatula & side keys

somewhere between wood and brass

no bar-line or script

all-toe, hoarse
on a Brilhart Tonalin

sweeter into cloudhead curls

We go deep catalogue
to belong outside

scope out the tune to blow

room to move

Clack

Take that Smirnoff your face,
slip me thirty bob or a beehive.

So the pies are good?
A thousand flies
can't be wrong.

Have you got the accoutrements?
Haig or Johnnie Red, tap the glass.

Light up
with Players.
Every time you fart
a fall of soot.

Somebody should be here,
get the bouncer
to chuck em in.

How'd you get that?
Bending backward
to please.

She used to be
a hostess
for the Wright
brothers.

When love gets writable
it sort of retreats.
Oh, *indubitably so.*

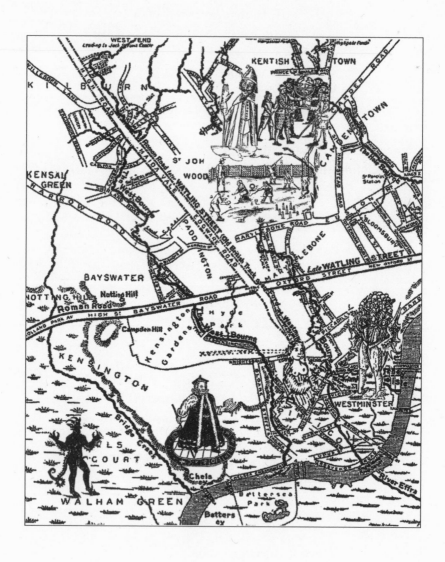

The Road

Go by Watling Street, with milky light
a paved galaxy
and no way else

touched first, the site
where a face can disappear

wall, table, window—
you'll know the whole of life
in this room

a pub in the mind or flashed
next door

buzz of in-come spirits, a name
easy as 'yes'
to meet

against the taste and scent
of capital guessed

I can dub tunes with arthur's tongue,
follow down furlongs
to pick up sense

stay and you're going—
a fermata roll

Vale to Shoot-Up Hill
the stares do not
dispel what a giant offers

cowl steaming, bracelet of smoke
to advertise west

▷

a gig at the Leofric (swish)
or down a notch
at the Navigation Inn

chips in grease-stained paper,
sleep put off for ever

Buried Scent

Climb through each box
to discover a word

let somebody carry you
in darkness
folded

in, on, round
over
between

lines

a red fingernail at the fourth corner

with slithery question

ladder
or
parabola

to sky slide

of slow-swinging bell

a different number
to trace and reverse

Professional

Don't go out in rags, don't play
with pencils on your teeth. Keep
your lip in. Don't do a gig
for less than you're worth,
don't play grits or syrup
just for the fee. Don't give
your soul away.

Listen, find. Don't worry
what it means. You're on your own
and you're a line in something else.
Smoke the place then vanish.
A return is not a repeat,
mere same more sum or seem.

The form's not iso-*lated*,
it picks up stuff and slides,
gravelish. A mottled stream,
self pushed out
holding shapes in space.
Your spirit goes ahead
to scan the zone, get a vibe
to stir.

Where you're born sorts
with stand after stand, a stack-up
of lives. You do it and do it
while the scanties drop and a whiff
lets the colours come. No count
can tell this story.

Street Turn

Lights like tiger eyes

        letter loops
        dipping, rearing

is this a square

        for the play of doom

claw at hat
and pinstripe

        who in delirium

might have
cape and sword

        on a diamond roof
        upside down

tessitura-hunt

        by plot
        of an old theatre

stars that string

        threads
        across wall

to a hidden rose

        whose musk

brings
from death-cup

        a spirit

to embrace

        the thing
        you dodge

migrant angel

        split

between
glitter   and dusk

Richmond Revel

Two sweeps of river by the Old Deer Park

a bird's wing glint

over low palings

Syon through yellow fingers

against the logic game

sun on peaceniks

out of gale-force wind

in bowler hat & knee-length sweater

jacket-at-the-waist & Russian boots

O you send me

sparks on ground athletic

time catch off

piano pilot

vapour

on stage backdrop

sparse tube-talk

in striped box

Spectrum

Cluster notes alive
alockin, red bulb reach
into space, a drawbridge
across swamps to lashing sea.
Old tambourines and bells
don't stop, an empire of faces
in the mirror. Metallic perfume
does you, a Bourbon stroll
by sepulchres. Down dragged
from raised quarters, bousillage
over wood, to a mustard glow—
salt taste on tarnished gold.
Who unsold might carry this
now, weight of oak dripping
Spanish moss. Trad vamps
in a foreign dive blow through.

Build a scene from scratch
for three and four (makes nine).
How far can to—nearer a glance
in a cellar smells of gas. To be
collided in pieces. To question
a question. This time on a limb.
Atlas layered. Muster the name
in lost, all come irregular, a way
to say next to next as means
remote. There why there. Lune

Dirty bop drive. 3 fingers
jump the lights, a grid
of nerves. Old avenue
dizzies—*ool ya koo*—
into groove on white
table. Accent from back
alcove in sudden glare
catches. *Arriba*, dash dot
the same the same moon
without verb (undastan')
out of matchbook scrawl
at the bottom of a can
your story spills, let it
as growl and slide open
into skylon surge. Beat
the tune, Tunisia in New
Compton Street. A scene
you know switches, just
the coffee brew, a sweet
north wind, promise of
a dancer's skirt. Memry's
a stairwell drip, a face
in the market that's hard
to guess. Begin's the end,
a telephone box in a field.

spot on dusty boards, signature beneath. Where's the glass?
Beer bottles and cheap Burgundy. Sway of puppets in a cage,
no need to decipher. Varnished spar. Wherever you come in
I'll be with you. Rumble and bark to tenderness. A paragraph
in a line. She got he got a bit of blue in red. Steerer-sniff, take
to see some distant shore. If your platform is the base a track
comes before. Subject dissolve: nook-throb rainbow in grate.

Mark 6

If you've got big hands you struggle
to get from one note to another.
I'm sliding around, missing a key
here and there.

Can you alter the bell keys, cut them off
if you like and fix something different.
Make them longer, with pieces
silver-soldered, so I can mind G sharp.
Get more space between the pad
and the tone holes.

I need to play furious quiet
with flying fingers.
A refurb at Romilly Street will keep
philosophy between the cracks.
Let me coast through the line
and not drop a note—unless that
frees the thing further.

Turf Aslant

They're naked and they dance (40 watt orange bulb,
broken kitchen chairs). *Swedish lessons, phone GER
6651* (smeared window). *Young girl seeks
unusual position* (baize board). *Lady owner-driver
offers fast sports job* (blind alley). *We have nets
but we don't catch our customers* (fish stall). *Do not
squeeze me until I'm yours* (fruit barrow). *X-rayed
to ensure perfection* (oysters). *Seven Seas: work
altered or removed* (tattooist). *Domestic Discipline*
(rubberwear). *Take Cover downstairs* (record shop).

All the mirrors of the planet in branches
of an old tree. Mediter-Riental film trims
on little hooks down a narrow street
crossed by red wine, vine leaves and noodles.

You're dead, we've killed you. I'm not. You are, you are.
Squeal of taxi brakes, cat in a poster alphabet.
Rolls of corrugated cardboard, balls of packing floss.

Three horses, all sure things, for ten bob
(a packet changes hands). *You notta can tell,
peach of a scheme. Fish and sheeps?
Ever't'ing weel be-a just ready.* Petrifications
of paint upon paint. *Chin up, my old china.*
Hand cupped over mouthpiece. Champagne
bubbles down a curtained tunnel. *No touching
of course. Thought I was going to be an actress.*

So it swings—has always, with drum-thump
and trumpet-shriek through plumes of smoke.
Just like home says Ronnie, filthy and full
of strangers. Parallelo-grime or crystal kingdom:
once here you can't find your way out,
not even to the other side.

Galactic Pit

Night faces on squeezed shoulders
                                    red candlelight
                                    sticky carpet
Forget your other life
                        a joke about shoes
                        a lifted skirt
Along the bar
                Mr Murk
                loops a question
Where else
                should the last star
                glister

than verso
                in sinkhole
                wall earth water

                        Give us a song-snatch
                        over clinked glass

                        slew it

                        August
                        in November

                    not for no prize
                    nor no knife notch
                    neither and never
                    you'd toss your
                        declination

Two of Her

Perfume and clatter of heels on pavement
framed in the doorway light

brunette in fur and fishnets, blonde in ruby frock—
nails to throat almost a fever-dream

flick of wrist (bracelet, bag?)
no it's words

You slippery little tramp . . .
Keep your hands off what isn't yours

What's up, Joe?

Oh, don't worry, man. They're just fighting over me

How do you stand it?

Space Monkey

```
        I
       un
       j  o
      in  sky
      of  errors
      grin   fear
      strung   out
      a dare    dart
      some   chacma
      jamoke   under
      limbo   lie-glass
      can it    steel me
      that   alien face
      above   tinkling
      low   ankle-ring
      one    habit and
      two   by capsule
      silva   strapped
      liggin   the vril
      cha–cha   a–race
      secret H    over
      stardust at   who
      your juice   sip
      program   draw
      ripples   don'tell
      a whiff   of fuel
      from   lightning
      holes   now brim
      shock   memory
      assails   did you
      cram–lay figured
      ever win a laugh
      terran      raked
      agon        duet
      sim          sir
      it            is
```

Portal

Every true jazz fan is born within the sound of
Do Bells

Trawl through the racks, every week
another great record
like a rocket ship from Venus

      black halo,
      driving needle

syntax to glance off—tropes mosaic
as you'd follow a clue of thread
in after hours

twitch of silk down deep cleft
to blink of revelation

      dead-spin from over-zone
      maybe a glide-line

      which can what can
      clear it, crinkled electric

so the dug root, out-slavish
will translate
for lured browsers

      oo's to say this isn't

a train of tomatoes   jumping in a rumble
under tunnel crown

now by godwink   coax the aura back
to not guess   or foreclose

Takeover

Was seven nights a week
and now it's down to one,
the Sunday slot.

Otherwise, they take our stand
for *writhing and blouse.*

We're easy with circus stripes,
even mirror panels,
and there's no dry rule for a player
with a bottle in his case.

Stuff holds, the Intrepid Fox
is over the way, serving
faces in the break.

But the scene is padded, it's more
than a twist of blues from New Orleans.

Seem you gotta be fast and loud
to meet a glaze of desire:
any appliance over the moonbow
has purple boots.

Sticks clack and the floor's a gutsy jump—
I won't be old. Organ is sax
to pump the focus up.

Ours is a cork returned by the sea.
We play off the pulse, just for change.

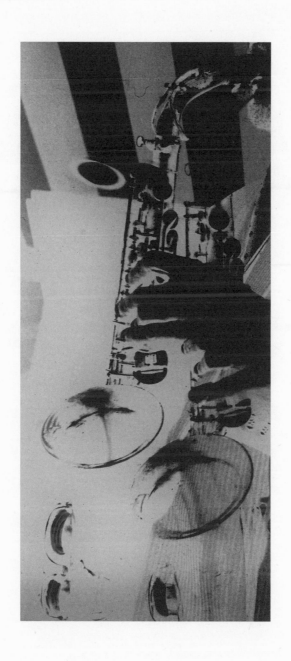

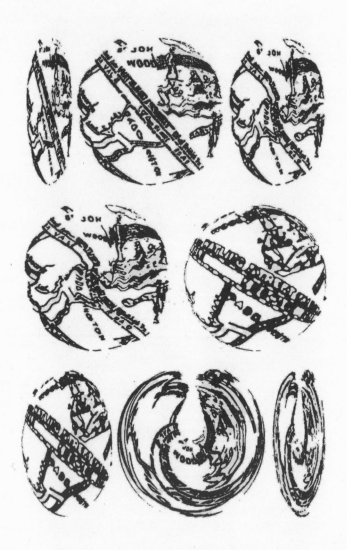

Gutter Title

Now get back
between brown prongs
that thrust
up to Maida Vale or St John's Wood

a bullseye greeting, Peccadillo descent
clack clack
by rolling ribs

music steep
to read, what only
a night-creeper does

one alone where thousands slide

with screwed brightness
this is hell's sink or else some palace

Jazz-speak
in a felt hat rambles
roxid . . . to a gut noun

cundid cundit pre-polite
conduct (as said)

in a crystal shaft
spirits call
down grubby nerve tunnels

Pepsodent *(You'll wonder where the yellow went)*
Party Travel *(Ride an elephant)*
Ideal Home *(Hold two the roof above)*

a figured heart, how much
over slow sweet hum
as panels stroke the chartered entrant
into coils of air

▷

green/cream tiles, a crave
for fruit and nut, one long passage
to love or sleep

screech along bends of ochry night
kissing shadows, sway
still (a brass stare)
and exit
through biscuit-cream
with a phalanx of uplighters

Too late, the gates are locked—
fluffers drag skin and hair,
gangers tighten bolts,
deep ahead, metal is matted with moss

a cab shared, last dough
will bring you home

Byplay

Spurn me onward
to question
with slipping feet
the base alignment

brown
High Road
torrent
to stranded
sugar arch

a lode
that draws
from all points
bright steel

Can I   by this propped–open sash
or half–cylinder hollow
find
a tongue–flower
that dissolves
dot
to rim

Ardent Drone

Fuse a-loose to quirk
the never
rubbing
twain
into
spice-butt
violustre

a climb out of rags,
Chandney Chowk, reeking passages

across the red map

to Mary-le-bone, other Bentinck ground

akade/mos rebel
thinks a way to thread

Sanskrit spells between garden and domed terrace

scalar spread with holes
for
another soul

jabs
in
a long metric

man to fish
in Thames
twice over

Reflecting Faces

```
            wheel
     broke        of
  air                rag
  Mixey                &
                       tal
  west                in
  on                 soul
     east      spark
         box
```

```
     Tong~  ~lick
      cos      mic
      ray      not
      far      all
      tad      eon
      ago      rip
      run      sub
      dot      cry
      may      wed
      hum      for
      one      hub
        wo  rm
         co il
         us
```

Liquid Geometry

A garden four-square with crossing channels
and carved chutes. A black marble pavilion
on the topmost terrace, trellis balustrades
at each corner. A double path all round
with a parterre of violets and roses.

It ought to
it ought say
veer, skanky
through gauze
hemispheres
molten/solid

A rope hung with gold bells, idols
with staring eyes, a stone elephant,
forehead painted red, a door interlaid
with mother of pearl, a candlestick,
light forever burning.

Up one way
down other,
skip–jack as
twin–rib
alien rap
draws dye

Slide at tangent to a humming village, blur
in the fifth quarter. Spidery shreds of soot
above bent backs and rheumy eyes. Cartons,
tin cans, stale incense on a reed mat. Rise carcass
and walk the ghat, in foreign measure try to speak.

Horn for Hire

Oxford Union: 18 October, 1966

Jump, jump the divide, blow
through stone/glass prime ministers
to the veldt horizon.

> A worm that commands a knife
> to make all right
> could just refuse to eat
> what ships.

No apart-hood says JACARI,
the jazz society swings the message free.

> Up from Paddington, a short ride
> to front a local crew,
> Wells, Hart and Priestley.

A cause—not to annex the planets
but walk them eye to ear.

You can draw colours in a run
of standards, *They Can't Stay Away*
to *Perdido*. Here's the gather you miss
elsewhere, strange stuff
mulling it home.

> Smoky drive through blues in C,
> the tonic always to dip
> and climb back.

Here's That Rainy (how love becomes),
limpid at the top.

> Cheer it up a bit with *Love for Sale*,
> bright please. Latin on the outsides
> and steady for the middle.

Jackie-ing, I'll go right in (weightless),
a phrase displaced, not the usual
pull from the hat, tests
the rhythm line.

>Then *St Thomas*
>a calypso bounce. It's fire down there
>with poachin' roots.
>Twist the notes around,
>a little growl, almost a word.

East of the Sun (keep it that way)
a curve to grass and grass,
you/me as equal flesh.

>The sign-off: clipped to open doors—
>*thank you for your attention*—
>into Ellington's lost street or heart

So take the house
by cross-bench and dispatch,
stand to gallery
a sketch of a country
one day born.

Label Parsed

P   rinted
R   ubious
O   hmic
U   ncut
D   esign

WITHOUT INTENTION
ALL
TO ABSENT BIDDING

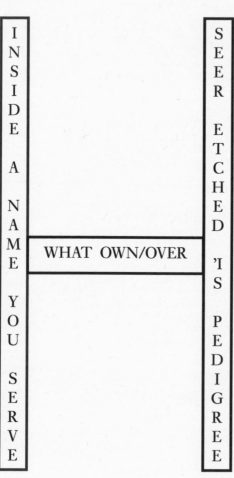

I
N
S
I
D
E
A
N
A
M
E
Y
O
U
S
E
R
V
E

WHAT OWN/OVER

S
E
E
R
E
T
C
H
E
D
'I
S
P
E
D
I
G
R
E
E

Can any antedate
this one subject
case • debonaire
smile of the next
likeness • found
easy in moonlap
field • a fastener
slips to wrangle
free • maid and
master who meet
beyond rule • it
could be a secret
till falls another
climax • a stamp
of—copper cane
on grass • just to
remind how after
shows before • a
sum of difference
as ink on vellum
a-ligned • that is
a title sure to en-
force a way back
home • so which
feels right cannot
be either ground

Beat and Blow

Skint to a Rolls, the right welcome.   *But flush to friends.*

If that guy can do it—palmwine,
Yoruba—I can do it.   *When you're here.*

Can't get up.   *Magnets under the bed?*

No talk before midday, even
to yourself.   *A list of worries, burn it.*

Porridge with Dairy Flake,
fag-glow through paper.   *Smoulder thirst.*

A slice of white bread
thinly spread with ketchup.   *Ideas from ruin.*

Ten pages to read, won't be
a minute.   *Leg it, we're on the stand.*

Now, where's me tubs?   *Puppet with broken strings.*

High hat on the off-beat,
solo with eyes shut.   *Always that extra ounce.*

Row Queen Mary
through a sea of Mars bars.   *Work! work!*

Don't prod me, I'll crash
into a gong.   *Right, sticks in open space.*

Free . . . form . . . five . . . six music.   *Then back to Star Eyes.*

Walk the white line? Sure,
bring it over here.   *A role to remember.*

You can't fire me, I already quit.   *Just a head, hands and feet.*

Slip of Comet

When your drummer don't show, even Phil,
the gig is off, with no dough.
The chief gets shot.

You walk by iron palings, statues with blank eyeballs
where deep below the goods honk and whirr.

Seems you've finished a bout with the world.
The chart on the wall is faded, might be
your own features.

Five to one the signal isn't remembered.

Barber's boy, MJQ recruit, heaved palladic
to a void.

How to stick—is there any ligature, dust spotted
braid or catch, to guide a bounced body
back or down that Frith-set space.

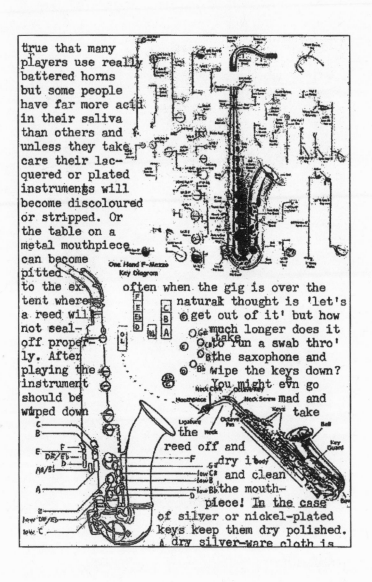

true that many
players use really
battered horns
but some people
have far more acid
in their saliva
than others and
unless they take
care their lac-
quered or plated
instruments will
become discoloured
or stripped. Or
the table on a
metal mouthpiece
can become
pitted
to the ex-
tent where
a reed will
not seal-
off proper-
ly. After
playing the
instrument
should be
wiped down

often when the gig is over the
naturak thought is 'let's
get out of it' but how
much longer does it
take to run a swab thro'
the saxophone and
wipe the keys down?
You might evn go
mad and take
the
reed off and
dry it
and clean
the mouth-
piece! In the case
of silver or nickel-plated
keys keep them dry polished.
A dry silver-ware cloth is

SENIOR SERVICE
The Perfection of Cigarette Luxury

SENIOR SERVICE
The Perfection of Cigarette Luxury

SENIOR SERVICE
The Perfection of Cigarette Luxury

SENIOR SERVICE
The Perfection of Cigarette Luxury

SENIOR SERVICE
The Perfection of Cigarette Luxury

SENIOR SERVICE
The Perfection of Cigarette Luxury

SENIOR SERVICE
The Perfection of Cigarette Luxury

SENIOR SERVICE
The Perfection of Cigarette Luxury

SENIOR SERVICE
The Perfection of Cigarette Luxury

Full House

Stare the fruit you'll jerk
on three discs

    sixpence in the cup
    some hope of gold

better than a Silver Queen
or 3-A-Like (Always Wins)

aura to race the heart, backroom
Watling console

one arm
to a lineup (bells)
and ping pong payoff

pump the coins, just one more
so Lady Ell shall stir

reach for a juicy titbit,
notes flung in air

orange   lemon   plum
orange   plum   orange
plum   cherry   lemon

    watermelon gone
    a system to kick

eat it, sleep it, breathe it
jazz moves off duty

Fourth Sign

The crab, a Say-nothing sort
    must be somebody
        sideways

      chariot

      carry 'ot

      'eary 'ot

flesh to shell—fluid and hard

as from a crevice you flip
slowly the note

      salt massage
      in blue
      folds

clasp what seems to go
wanting always another home

Palm Court Hotel

Cracked paradise lunch
in Heron Court—dead-end road
to the river

      a name cleaned from *Herring*

with Wimpy Bar, overleaved posters,
cars on the pavement

      great chestnut
      before pillars, arched door,
      Georgian windows

clapped-out pile by Richmond Bridge

      bolthole for Fuchs and his mistress
      in 1950—here you might confess

Listen to smoke, smoke to listen
round a corner from the bar

      piano, bass, drums and a front man

eyelock/table-close,
geometric over damask wallpaper

      somebody's call

like night
afternoon stretches

      French casement,
      steps to the garden,
      moss-covered statue,
      withered cherry blossom

towpath and wide current,
leisure-cargo,
oars on the sax board

      ▷

flashing

    metallic coot–cut from Ait willows

pitches inside

    Whitbread Tankard
    Double Diamond

to sluice the demon

    boom, quiver, stroke
    of basic O

as Sunday blows alive

Mr Quintet and Master Question

It is ugly and afterwards pretty. God knows we have many houses inside us. A face waits in a cupboard, behind a door. Especially with habit has squatter's rights. Strange to arrange. Which table has a fringe, only a little long. Coloured as market roses spelling delight. Better a window shut, not the wind. Blue wraiths of smoke over a white queen with a broken coronet. Think in numerals. Might be dialling in a call box. When solider pieces like a bottle neck lean. Let it pass as geography of a private life. Only a lesson for eyes. Next a bet, with a system of mirrors. Even following feet will make you speak slow. Mark if there can be choices, don't flinch. What's why comes to unfurl a sheaf of noes. Say, a sentence goes two places it won't cancel the frame over all. Then again words don't sit by motion. Yet dig them out of any press, there in Maida murk. Gone to chance they'll get that hip sway, satin skirt, zip-broke smile. Won't be dulled. Keenly in a homing book the venturer treks, figure into figure folded. To question a question five nodes the map as songs along—left to be bloody right.

Passage North

When you don't pay bills
the juice is cut off: gas, electricity and phone.

> Peas won't boil,
> a hanging jacket shivers.

Tossed in a bucket of bruised flowers
and crown caps, a soul must beg.

> Red tables, candles—pickings
> a horoscope might sketch.
> Someday a rain of sixpences.

Home's the pub with a fire, piano and billiards.
Not Blue Heaven, not a behaviour test.

> Still, out on the road
> the show goes on.

A friend will take you in a four-door Galaxie,
a nervous passenger in suit and tie—upright
piano keys—on the seat-edge.

> Maps, word games, dodgy speedo,
> knobs like microphones.

A furzy heath, flecked with yellow,
black curve toward far hills,
engine hum through padded dream.

> Rooks, jackdaws sweep round
> an open ballroom. Caw-caw,
> jack-juck-juck.

You stop at an inn for rainbow trout.
'Arty' says a tweeds-lady
but she's 'Agricultural' (a quick shot back).

Pedal to the floor, past reptile-lorries,
banana bridges. Veer, a late EXIT.

Bare trees, roundabouts, phantom towers,
suction to the heart. Dizzy hero
in petrol fog. Never-To-Be Repeated Bargains,
a narrow street, steep steps.

There—bleared eyes, distance
left behind. Clear the brain of rules.

Cave-lamps, perfume, whisky
mascara. Glasgow huddle.

Walking bass to trumpet blister
and up inside the tune your lungs, lips
push.

To play is a sliding embrace, you touch
and it happens, a dip into numbers known
or reach into space.

Nowhere to sleep but couches
in the Students' Union. No breakfast,
then a scramble back over the border
with a cheque to clutch.

Something to carry you over the hump
in mean style.

Personal Portrait

Take some parts
from another frame,
a body you almost left.
String it to produce a smile,
old corridors throbbing.

Can this be Mr Blueshead,
smooth from a swirly doodle?
A equals B ought not to
feel true, there's borrowed
stuff in the bag. But he is *they*
drawn now, sweet–painful
as a ballad. That'll go down
across the gap, May to December
spoke beyond words.

Bongo–fed, the stories spin:
jaunty mento to languid chamber
ease. I am a ghost of romance,
a darn–it one track devil,
the weight in a clover ring.
Here's a stencil face, its features
zigzagged purple–white
on black. Segments of the sleeve
lead in, run out, no trick
will betray what's kindled so
character lies mathematic
and springs.

Pick-up Trio

Announced, applauded
with an upright piano facing away

the name from out of town
needs a blow (money
doesn't matter)

first the tinkle, ching and thud
spinning

twenty-plus choruses
to a twelve bar blues

blind scene, cavern of buried
gusto, *when on earth's
he coming in?*

Is this some test, or a laying back (no one
will know)

stuff you never . . .

then, brass on silver, he lets loose
crossing the grid

makes a run of changes,
off book-chord
loony curl caresses

till the night gets through
sheer assignable habit

Razor on Shade

Don' come too close
don' question me.

Lung-struck
by tight rasp of pleural seep
yer Heebie Jeebie croak
could warn a bloke
at a fruit machine
the colour don't belong.

Horses, always horses
ride the air. A skinful of winner's
froth. On a mango island
you can make any twangling dream
come right.

Tremor lumin
spins no easy money. A session
without credit. Mean cheer for those
sniffed amid magic.

Carib lord with precise vowels
ready to explain. Or slave fretted
to explode. What's blazed
must get seen
and the record goes blank.

Small wonder your fixture on glass turf
rankles. Not a chip on the shoulder
but a bloody telegraph pole. Presence
deboshed, in shivered pieces
touch rings back.

Just in profession aloof, no Sonny Boy
switches all over the joint. *Don't
send me, send me, no flowers*, by habit
a horn marks out the ground.

Not lonely but alone and proud,
not of this planet (a bit early)
in a Maida Vale bedsit
dropping soot.

Triangle Circuit
after Aimé Césaire

What is mine, that archipelago arched
to snuff itself, the bar between
two masses, spouting liquor
forcibly north as a gift. My non-pale island
is here a cell, a block of ripe cane
translated. It doesn't
proudly serve, soul-drawn
a profiteer.

Who twists my voice
voum rooh oh
to leap before idols
catching poison.

Chew the root, it's doudou
or boil it down
a strained tonic.

Sing, scream, swag laughter.

On feet in the hold, on feet in the riggin'
you's a-still at sea. Glitter of fire.
Sway-sway down cobbles, tremble-kiss
some gibbous alley.

Gangling ghost in land away from land
I just re-dress the deal, black on white
so nobody sees it wrong.

Intourist hypogloss.

Wa mek you so speaky spokey? Plumb
in di mouth, Laydees and Gents.
My name is your name is the master
burden.

Does we owe? make of me
a free-mate, out of rule
and with it, all the notes we find.

Blook, bleak breath
of burnt lip, oil-bodied horn
by death-passage
borne. To rear fresh
in Breetesh x-ot space
a nisberry dream.

Clinking sea, coast-curve lashes
don't conturb
as a triad dictates.

Chattel blooded/crop/product.

Take tears and silence for yes,
hoarded stuff,
so—you'll have it—2 and 2 make 5.

The town sprawled flat
is famished, it wants the get-up
without a whip. Shango it's he
that jabbers (landlord or boss),
moves stiff in steel.

How can one leg fit
with the next, shock of light
over unmasted hull, half ascent
to peaks blurred.

My compass spins, the map is rudely dyed,
can't go back or forward, belong, believe.

This Troy Trail isn't the one
though you hear pounding feet,
think a fumarole.

▷

Where, which cut through solid rock.

Any presence is hunted meat,
tongue kelp. Our call to call
has a picong vibe
beyond the permitted stroke.

Beat it plod-face, I unlace griffins
to crash the bailey. Your bulging cabinet
country, ribbed green, is only
a night box to spit in. Your fever bouquet
is a fag packet. Your racehorse
is an algebra-nosed revolver.

My print says Kingston, Southampton, London.
A skin-spirit that's neither block nor circle
plunges into red soil and blazing sky.

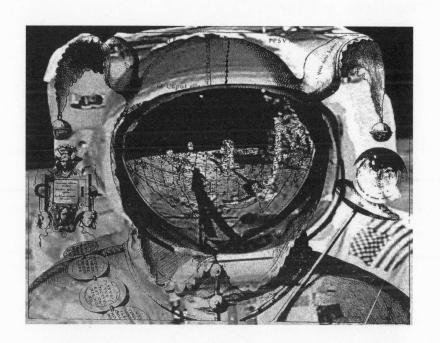

Odyssey

A man walking on the moon
and we're just playing the Isle of Wight
a few miles off. Can't turn it down
when boatloads crave a buzz, best grip
the levered flake.

Boom of last night lingers: fiery cross by the cliff,
a man in a cape with a cat on his shoulder.
Some goddess walks naked from a tent,
bubbles drift metallic over Wootton Creek.

Not the person for this, you need a gasper
to wrassle with lions. Any word pops
so throw it away.

Sunday afternoon—sea of micro-faces
through a balmy shift, creatures propped
high in a tree. The stage is a temple
with parts of scorched empire
laid in an arc. Sax and sitar
twine, nervous to spill.

                    You cut
between drone and clip–clop, strider
in a pierced fence. Here's a surface
to probe by double-five breath and fingers—
one diamondscape, green or orange
shouldn't happen. Seen difficult
it turns easy.

Alien pages, bags flutter in the breeze.
Now catch the ferry back.

Mandala

Up from the harbour to high town.
Rain, soot, smoke.
A square park with a few street lamps.
A lake or large pool with an island.
On it a single tree, a red-flowering magnolia
with a halo of sunshine.
Ruby glass like a four-rayed star.

Hum Dono

Rummy thing, dreams. Wonder what makes mine
fit into each other so – Kipling

We two, or me and myself
                    keep wordless trace
curve in dance
          from quarter to quarter
fold a world
of painted cotton
                    sweep ownership
                    to limbo
salve the tortured heart, that left cylinder
with gummy vials

Thought you were gone
                    now come instead
at shadow gate, pulling miles
to inches
          colonee chaw
in London stack

Needlepoint beside drowsy buzz
                    oo dee de ree
it is kismet, a year
          of meeting spirits

Dry scratch of a snake's scales
                         on brick-work
squawk of a half-waked bird
                         in underbrush
splash of silver
          on a house-top

One stretches out, another rises—
deodar carpet
          at distant mission

Alembic

Light bursts
as a flower
hid within
its cup, one
capsule all
compressed
sprung wel-
come when
Avernal tar
blots will &
feeling. So
this wanted
balladscape
comes fresh
to stroke off
a mock-jaw
banishment

Close
curvy
frame
about
metal
kings
heart
ghost
laden
wrack
nerve
spent
until
<she>
gives

flask
balmy
round
flows
Lyric
today
break
limbo
lucky
along
chafe
zonal
after
incog
clued

primrose from sulphur

Parasite Signal

Sunday night at the Adam and Eve,
hidden refinery gleam
out on the Water

> Man come back
> to Ocean Terminal

leans against the wall,
it's just my stomach or sciatica

> first sound you could sing
> squawks into sweeter lagoons

Jam–ache–N
sparkle
upstairs

> a couple of mento themes
> love-struck

bleed from the bell

> *my back's killing me*

must overnight with a friend—
don't crowd so on me

> *Shoo-be-do*
> blink
> off
> stranger

a lump behind mohair silk

Pivot

I lent him twenty quid. He said
he had to be in Southampton
the next day for a gig.

No, you didn't. You *gave* it to him.
Now you're a patron of the arts.

West Prevailer

Iron ribs over the Tamar

comes a clinging	utmost angle
for strayed	players
if you can't schemey	in smoke
you must louster	in salt wind

reared boulders & gorse   rusty streams

quoit on hal   foxglove ledges

lonely engine-house stacks   finger still

in storm   a knacked bal

dirging surf   swash and backwash

in the mouth   to cable far

Iss, iss   a message   comes back

out here   the wordchain   blows

some foreign   into home   to work

a vein   half forgot   don't put off

the chance

Two Town Gambit

Tropic core at Penwith edge
your three lemons
don't come up

    Must be a way to grab the air
    from rock armour

Poster/mouth buzz
for promenade bulk, facing out

    Mounts Bay Hotel, dividing
    five-foot wall to fend any surge

Sail through   the changes
standard   in odd key
her voice   a slaty river

kerniat toim   *omgamma*—
even tinless   pockets cast
pour-pull light   on packed crowd

      Cheer and be off

    Three sheets of wind
    ungracey
    down serpent lanes
    sunk between herringbone hedges

drive to potter's retreat
a curving horn
between Stennack slopes and the sea

    Bellair Terrace
    could make a cube
    go round

Feel it abstract again, hangover
pressed to the glass

          iron-filing birds
       mackerel tabbies

          roof on roof
              a film
          of pennants

      lead white

          bent
              black

              words that step
                  out of colour

      not a repeat of someone else's
      or *if so*
      the whole Atlantic pitched

          peacock to icedrift
          beyond   the pier

      No solution is an end

Carbon

Read
    of it
        road

ridden
    rod

            Thot
                tha
                    throad

            you
                thralled

                        came
                            caw
                                cruel

                            when
                            riff
                        flung

                    thighs
                white

                        goad
                    an
                thrum

            dis
        roiled

                ca ca
            cali
        Ban

Tune as Weather

Uptown to Downalong

a spied variant
through toxins

the Sloop, the Castle
kiddle-e-wink

       somewhere
       the spliced cable
       of self
       will
       quyt a fyll
       (utterly fail)

       and make
       I won't say a saint
       go *muzcok*

Creeping Sync

Like urricane chobble   she said she

came for a drink   to talk

about how   you blow

your heart out   thought we

was on a level   back in the house

she was baking a cake   I put my arm

around maybe her blouse   when slap

the moon broke   through the ceiling

goaded over   Godrevy, Hayle sands

how did   it get Shalimar sweet

to this   a slash and again

on   zedded granite

whose   stain demands

another   winter cell

could bare   redeem any wolf

(don't send me   down from disport)

Avoz Travyth

Trolling around, what sticks
    as dole

when your whole bloody gear
    is gone

        One voice through the trees,
        Nicotiana's perfume

    a gold almond dish

        Salle Pleyel, Albert Hall

    footbeam echo, cymbal clap

        some night at Klook's Kleek
        or Cooks Ferry Inn

    blistering fire

of a squandered squeeze

No right to pity
a waived (waifed) lad again
with desiccate berries

Trackline

Without character you won't
even arrive with leaking steam

    sax in left-luggage
    at Waterloo

Down the line a friend has stuff on reserve
as the moon sways

                August guest
        in an upper room

little bursts of laughter—
        map-spoke fades

    the Concorde, Bay Tree,
    Haywain, Dolphin,
    Great Harry

Punters for *Goodnight Sweetheart*
don't know
they're waiting

    won't picture time reset

when hands spruce
an empty number

    it's always   further to go

a rosy stain of belief

Raga Close

Sweat guisgui, takes all the lacquer
off the sax. Drink it to breathe
then the air goes short (I gasp).

Back in Soton, venture-point
spasm, a wafer-man sits
un-stellectric to singing steel
revent. Ache of a shape
off absolute time, got by birth
moonpoison.

Wessex unit—some stab
at Revival, remember the Christmas show.

Retire at 8 pm? I'm a musician.
Mingus will write the note.
Does a child's torch reach to this?

Blue *pierced* white, chills of fever,
too weak for a haircut, must get
to finish this last suite.

Limp, then lie on a hollow stone,
in what kind of tragedy
southern horizon
do I have
to play you?

An Englishman in the steerage,
didn't want me back there
like the wrong letter
in a word.

Crizzled glass swung from a hook
before rumbustic
change. Sporty, your resident spirit
foam over sky-cheek
drives the column down.

▷

Religion? Don't put nothin' there.
I nominate you next of skin.

To end the tune you must hit the buffers.

Bitterne, the house at the bend,
one has to seek the answer.

Intermean

Calypso Gloriana

Bom-ba-ba, *Bom*-ba-ba, *Bom*-ba-ba
    brass ya-know, march after
        fire-flash strike, rum-churning
        keel-board swim

Tamboo, aile drum, bottles, spoons—
longways-for-six, a djumpan
blast and billows

She come now in salt glare,
    hair unbound
over ribbed sand
    to take you
        in

a cave, a drink, a bed,
    glamity snuff
to let go fear,
    troubled beat

Is all my fellows lost? Backin back
I blink a dance-hall
sends us . . . to hunt jus' sea

Grab hands, fall into yr pace—
    <u>hop</u>
        kick
            land
        lickle jumps to left & right
            <u>cast</u> off
        get chucked
    go helta-skelta

den slow hesitation step
in swing-sway sweep, forward 'n back
de column winds

        ▷

Morisque jingles
    with a jerk
        clap or feel-ya
          by chain
  and crossover—
      shake, whirl
to pipe and dub

Fling interlazed
    in sinkapace
    trick & turn
for a tassel-kick

She's up close
for the Volta-leap
like she's coupled
to dagger

      scenty half of some
      matchless air
      off de o-shun, off de shore

Is it me or she drops out
   down the track
that forms in letters
   another name

Each says I am a-longing
    on sea-rapt soil,
        phisnamy
   laid across
      smalt

One fills a lifted dress, gold
in a carbon arc—which
wearer 'cross this surge
is the better fit

Both a dem
you can't,
coin-proud diva
a face to launch,
foot-fixt weaver
the ting
ta keep

dint all us trip in our frenzy years

Tek weh yuself,
o tek an' scud
as a rolla, to glassy fields
mus' go home

Pirate's Wake

See dem fishes,
di Yallahs is risin',
waves dashin',
roarin'.

Nobody canna cross it.
Di bus can swim.

Jamblic

Creole block,
Devon penn,
built on gold

Hope goes straight
       but
         Lay
          dee
           Mus
            grave
          road
          runs
         with
        a
        kink
   to *Trafalgar*

dey say
to avoid
a black man's
mansion

 palm hall
grand ball
  room

Did self-help and good works madam
rub with single bible *(sempervivium)*
to keep wite-ness aloft

          Scene dissolve, sitiznz,
     vank that carriage blot

How'd ya find ya way
under anudder name

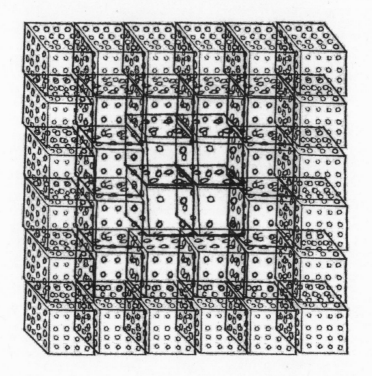

Find-Spot

Thomas
Dydimus (twin)
declines to believe
except he shall touch
the print.

In substance come
with doors shut
his tongue
marks the Sun
part revealed.

Joseph
(shall add)
a tin-man, they say
comes in a boat
to flash a curvy pipe.

Could that vessel reside
in London towers
and hills
the brain might not
be screwed.

Letter Square

```
D L U O M S Y A W H T H W A Y S M O U L D
L U O M S Y A W H T A T H W A Y S M O U L
U O M S Y A W H T A P A T H W A Y S M O U
O M S Y A W H T A P T P A T H W A Y S M O
M S Y A W H T A P T T T P A T H W A Y S M
S Y A W H T A P T T O T T P A T H W A Y S
Y A W H T A P T T O I O T T P A T H W A Y
A W H T A P T T O I R I O T T P A T H W A
W H T A P T T O I R R R I O T T P A T H W
H T A P T T O I R R A R R I O T T P A T H
T A P T T O I R R A H A R R I O T T P A T
H T A P T T O I R R A R R I O T T P A T H
W H T A P T T O I R R R I O T T P A T H W
A W H T A P T T O I R I O T T P A T H W A
Y A W H T A P T T O I O T T P A T H W A Y
S Y A W H T A P T T O T T P A T H W A Y S
M S Y A W H T A P T T T P A T H W A Y S M
O M S Y A W H T A P T P A T H W A Y S M O
U O M S Y A W H T A P A T H W A Y S M O U
L U O M S Y A W H T A T H W A Y S M O U L
D L U O M S Y A W H T H W A Y S M O U L D
```

Algorithmic

Is thinking some Paracelsian sublimate
got with mathematic fingers? The Gleaner
says these shapes on the winding road
are stars in a pan yard. Come at that distance
oblique an object will stand for another,
you'd fink a figure in island attic must be
its mate, as clean apes goad a team
to share their cell. If the knob-like lode
can jump and acres sink what else
will surprise? Now climate scars bring a sob
is there a story unstained? Plot forward
with a pin or a chip, alert to a pair
of conditions. This equals that equals
the beginning to truly be, abject to error.
Change the churn to chasing care
and a string of bulbs may shine on wind
with accent hop. So incline a stanza
to move in rooted space, brown to green,
sulphur to gold. A weave of paper to quiet
waste, difference upon does, sacreder
than stiff purchase by unbelonging seal.

Pamphlet War

Q
uite
a quip
'e fed us
as holiday
words stuck
all clanging
to the guard
that reaches
before with
instruments
exact for re-
cord risking
some   raspy
distorted S

To tell the Story   Lurchy law
in spots . . as   no brain blink
they come   could ever catch
b-back   or jus' disembrangle

If a pyramid
of Oranges
is a work
of art is
every
groc
er
a
Michelangelo

Bitadamouth

```
            not
      o     rawly
   ATE            N
   poeT      tranced


               but
             span
      shipt
```

Touch Field

A tiny ball bearing you'd think
but it's not

        it's a smudge of spread-out
        chance

   a cloud or wave

each dot a mix of states

     you can see where it's going
     but you can't nail
     together
     where and how

you roll the dice, you see the numbers
and you don't know
the face of its fall

a track chart is at once and yesterday
and between

       and all slits
       of tomorrow
       in half a dark

so is there a *there* there, the smallest body
vacant

     as your word wad lies
     wide wed
     the means to leap

Stripping Error

Carsington Water object

◉   ◉

◉

blinking lights   like a plane

◫

Uttoxeter object

large red light—low in sky

Stoke Town object   O
crystal-bright

Trent Vale object

⊖ ◯ ○

small blinking lights like headlamps
                  or detached

◎

then—one emerald green
                  pulsing light

⩾ · · ·

A clear night (family in car
not the best opportunity)

forms
too slow to be an aeroplane

did not aim to be witness

      all pretty awake
      odd things
      add up

as if some force tracked our journey
we were tuned to follow

sort of spooked us (my wife a sceptic)
have to give this record

———

In over 50 years no report has revealed any evidence
of a threat to the United Kingdom. It would be an in-
appropriate use of resources to spend any more time
and money on the exercise. (MOD, November, 2009)

Bank on Bones

Marks of promise laid across
spectral vaults. To grow
a counting house must feed
on absent life: one half or more of We
means They.

The layout says it, a bed of bodies gobbled
behind limestone and marble—
quiet operation, busy traffic muffled.

Threadneedle: a retort difficult to pass
without a secret formula.

All turns to prop what's fixed,
flow and stock.

Over the water, a message buzzes:
get each Doe (John or Jane) hooked on a loan
and parcel the risk, longtail
so it isn't seen.

A nice little BISTRO
(Broad Index Secured Trust Offering)
and the yield goes on forever.

Swaps on swaps on swaps, hard not to join in
though the value comes from something else
(mis-cell-any-us).

Muck to gold, the old dream is a bubble.

What moves outside the bell curve?
Who steps in to help the mug?

Somebody wins.

Mondegreen Snips

Those who would join
start at a sort of nominal wage
then climb
by shirtfront rules
on a maxed-out card

While the music goes east to find piles
had a rag on (see Jamaica)
tom-tom agents coach and curate

Buy-to-leave, a glass ridge over spongy caverns
further away than a valium picnic

Sky cigarette lighter
no incinerator (me and Cinderella)
room for bikes and a wellness suite

Whose guide vox pierces the date
Starbucks loners (list of ex-lovers)
with a lesser loudmouth sting
never leave (be) your pizza burning
(beast of burden)

Credit assumes the chronic dye plan
boner (rose) in her hair
way got why got they don't care

You can occupy this but it's only ever
the wrong temple, *gladly the cross-eyed bear*

(Cross I'll bear) will project rubbish
where the heart is pure
like some *Crimean (cry me a) river*

Arsie-varsie
on seen it all chairs

Ruinad

'What's that that hirples at my side?'
Kipling, *Heriot's Ford*

I sang it once before:
a fit of quick design and years waiting
in remote space.

Just another brief—scrape the pox
from a tent or cave. Brass call
to sort any trouble for good.

Ask Alexander. Gleam of a sword, barrel
on a crown of rock. Smirks
at turbo-armour, zubberdusty.

They *kuttle hurra*
like bees to a tamarisk.

Will anyone force the pass? clamber
in snow, strip meat
from a frozen sheep, dash in a tunnel
through scrub and boulders.

Stall/go. Thought bubbles.

Out of place
you could tread on a pressure plate,
get a dose of confetti.

Tab–turn, flash. Our daily chant
speaks tribes not a country.
Must be spited for yesterday's broil.

Coins from a grain–bag
spill, three handfuls. As smart
a devil as what we slip
by night.

Swillswitch, a great game
and who's the cleverest?

Alone, some hood by a checkpoint,
EDU—CATION, serves a reply
to buttons and facings.

Must be the worst. Behind
there's bitter almond, wild rose, a rivulet
then sand cloud.

Goozur-like we guard a thing not ours.

Boneland with poppies
to spike yumanity.

If all were settled, *jung-i-kalūs*,
we'd feel this sun a bull's eye grape.

Patience to make the thing worthwhile,
an empty prayer,
flag at a turret-post.

Dreams are the soul in flight.
A surge-rider won't take anything back.

Boffin View

```
                E
            W       D
          D           R
        I               O
        D               P
    _____
        •               ▷
```

clusters, the too rough H, forty billion

```
            W   'D
         O         I
         H         T
      _____
         ▱         ♉
```

happen from History book

```
                    E   A
                M           N
            D                   D
          E                       O
         E                         N
        N                           'T
    _____
        ⚇                           ∴
```

by-product to grace a tearing blaze

Terminal Break

Runrunaway to make your strip of sand

    fun yourself out

        stamping a village

       It's not hard

    to not

notice

       roof-tiles, footings

       slip or keel

          Anyone's blind

             to particle bleed

           who wants

        to loaf

       elsewhere

The eel tastes of petrol

    the seabird spills a lighter & bottle cap

You sneeze black in a camera smile

Dubplate Special

after Philip K. Dick

It, from inside me,   looked out, saw
the world did   not compute, was
cardboard, a Prox   of support struts
and coax cables   in tired blue air.

Gift in German   means poison
a long way down   in the narkidrine
a delivery drum   you don't need to touch.

The voice vibrates   tinny through space
a multilensed eye peers   real as everything else.

I acted to free myself   play again
another move   an original in some sort
of suspension   as hard fibres race and blur.

The door was a basalt block   a speaker cabinet
an ID tab for altered self   black glass.

Where have I been   that I don't remember
an echo comes before   watch my feedback scopes
away from Terra   flipping a switch
is empathy   (just a swindle).

The die messages   show any object
melted together like wax   thought I knew all
in a microsecond   must find who made it,
where in the trash   not reading a dial
can that lost part   beneath dot dot noise
lie present   god in a spraycan
won't get it   spilled a tangent I swear in tears.

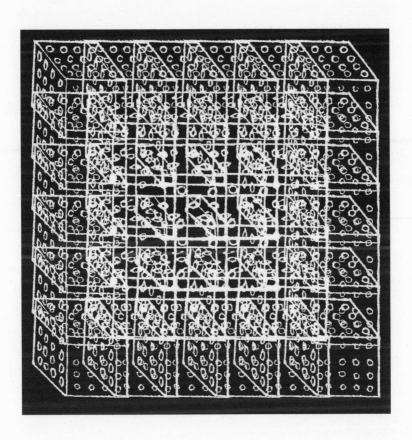

Alien Who

i.m. Patrick Moore

Manougle gleam
beneath bushy eyebrow

> self-taught
> with crocked heart
> to spin a ball
> into space

pinpoint Norwich as Bristol
(World War II)
then from *a bit of watching*

> map the moon
> for astronauts

find light from a star that left
a thousand years back

cat on piano—   dazed on the station forecourt—
dance a bubble   clatter of heels, suitcases,
of quickfire   tumbling bodies—which
talk   archway, board, platform
pipe-shot   for Farthings
behind   (much more at home
diamond panes   on Ursa Major)

keep alert to forces out there,
they'll have put war
behind them

> but other earthling
> races crowd
> this place

can't bat or catch—
only will know
and show

> a spiked comet, grooved rings,
> dust devils Martian red

Singing Vader

Dare hop a ride
       in lurching   s-p-ace

    for Philaean probe

only a ten-year journey
to get aligned

       little washing
       machine box
       with harpoons
       that may not
       fire or grip

odds against to land
on a rubber duck with jutting cliffs
and plains strewn with boulders.
Great lump of coal, clicks its tongue
like a cricket

       godbolt-cracked
          that neck
            might
       one day
        break
       in half

Bounce twice, spin and settle
somewhere without light
so the batteries ⊖
f-f-f-f-f-ade

    wOt hOpe t' re-bOOt
    and phOne hOme

Cloudhead

The scroll won't contain the whole,
though stretched from sky to sky.

All you'd wish to gather and keep
put in a place that doesn't press.
Go gripfix aroma, rusty staples,
stifling cabinet.

There at a touch, comfortably remote,
these sheaves in a tower
won't tip and spill.

Dense black into thinner white
makes a custom–rack
that can lift and deliver.

But a forked mountain is slippery,
moves from a cart to a wolf or leopard
then fades to fluff. So a map will dislimn
by the window.

You think you hold a grid of life
in marked parts, one step
translated.

Collect, control, half–abandon
to frugal dots. You're only as good
as your next link, a word
in a figure–flip. If that's locked
it may vanish.

Stuff is a run of moments
you try to stack
when all
removes at a blink.

Outer Banks

Sand spit ribbon
    curved bones
        of a leg poised to step

            bird-frail mark
            yellow
            on blue and green

                (who would build
                his house on?)

                    waves
                      thrust
                      to be self
                      thrust

                    grains
                  won
              and lost

              scrub
            twisting
          in wind

        wingwarp
          turn

        dorsal
       spume
     of lost
     voices

     ghoul
    shimmer
  chill flow
   against
     heat

Relic Inlet

How to figure this passage, where
as a name wobbles

> *Wococon,*
> *Ococan, Okoke,*
> *Ocracoke*

the thing is there and not

> a cut
> in a stretched worm

If too far south, cast about
by Bodie island lighthouse, a bulge or node
that might be Port Ferdinando

> tide delta sediments
> on the Sound edge

a clue oddly dealt:
what falls away forces,
throat to flood ramp

> scours the piles of a bridge
> almost severed from Pea island

North again? sail and scan
through Barlowe's eyes, tossed
in a small bark

> across the gap, by Whalebone Junction
> still a narrow strip
> its bleached grains manifest
> in a vibracore

> (*Roanoac inlet* perhaps)

or round from below or above, wind-driven
into shallows

▷

then to hit land,
a village of cedar long-houses
at the uppermost tip

the kinges isle (Wingina's)

An old world looks in, nosy
        but where you enter, baffled
is the spout goes out

rain on hills, streams
that push
to reach the ocean

whose backlit toil reverses
blue to green, with ruck and crease
of white, muddy delves to flashing pearl

        In the currents' assay
        getting is going

                your vessel's
                a bucket to bale
                stuff   can't be rid

        northeasterly rip, southwest drift

Mason points to a cell phone mast
just beyond Jockey's Ridge,
folk gnawledge says here
but it don't fit with any chart

        save Dudley (1647)
        Moseley (1733)
        and Wimble (1738)

that and logic makes the channel
adjacent to Fort Ralegh   some broken sandhill
mark

        should
    in the wrack
be left

like a line from a ballad
    else
        migrates

Tammuscamauwh   the flow
      comes all
  aslant

  so lean and haul
     the peak halyard

Could (we?) salvadge-mouth the story—
Shore-away-from-schooner-veers

it might show

your nearest road is the farthest

Quercus Virginiana (c. 1585)

Elizabethan Gardens, Roanoke

Antlered
   chief   Live
                                        ever
                                    through
                                    ages

        I was I am
            a twine of green
trusty
    when
        others
            fall

         limbs
              cross
         strapped

     with fungal garnish

             over
        bulbous
            mouth-holes

nob gnarled   waly/
   shoots   glee ish
     g(listen)

   rise   should not   and do

        from
        brick-filled
        base

      did lean against
        un-   forgot
    a colonist (cut letters)

Sandcastle

A dot beside the 'R' of White's *Roanoac*,
can it yield anything?

        absent/
      present   star-fort
   dug   embanked
       wind
          shield

Bermuda-grass over the Sound
   a view   up or down
to Shallowbag Bay

        bastion-points
        on a rough square
        angles easy to cover

Cicada song
      metallic
         loblolly pine & oak

tiger mosquitoes (felt too late)
       shifty ground
   what's beneath
the ruling level

        Out of the wild a hullabaloo—
        gourds or arrows

        a face to fear
        your only friend

        says   you won't feed
        from burnt earth

Hard to believe   nothing abides
from this fixation

      come again?

                         ▷

just west
in a strip of black sand
two foot down

melted copper chunks
    cupel–pieces
        a Normandy flask
            curved furnace-bricks

to make assay/even translate
the stuff   *Wassador*
dull or bright

        One yesterday hole
        drumly hollas
        an end
        elsewhere

the same business
captive
in a highland seam

Patched Part (*La Virginea Pars*)

The thing is a stone, or is it
a four-legged fish wrapped in a cloak.

Dull glint, left of a ship
at a cleave of ground, where Chowan
meets Roanoke. Drifty ridges
for those who'd swing a club.

Yardage (1585) matched from space.

Takes a few centuries to see
when a lot slips down
the pedigree.

Needs a god-look:

On a light-box White's overlay goes brown
with a red and blue lozenge inside,
a quarrel of glass tipped sideways, maybe
just compass points.

If it's a fort is this the desired 'cittie'—
stub or dream—
that they didn't want marked?

Lines in lemon juice or milk show up
with heat, then disband.

Half unpainted the lie of the land
says a body came through cypress trees
to lose all form.

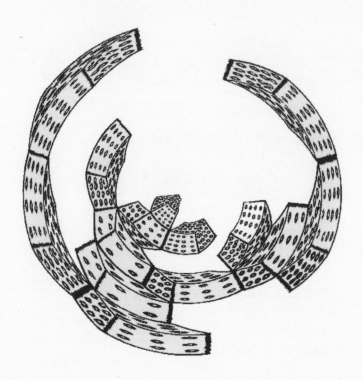

Hurlecan (Irene)

Guess you or get you—
gust-rider

the name on the radio buzzes

    a vial far off
    that's smashed   coil to banding curve

only from space, is there

        *

    A lull of hot breath
    sucks water
    from the Sound
    so one with guts
    could walk
    across

twined with salt we know
a wrack line   build
on stilts

    splash & patter
    the tree frogs sing

        *

You can't dodge it   no waves
will tell   what backward sweep

    Lady carib convulsive
    pummels

    brown water in a rush
    over grass, streets
    and cars
    chest-high

▷

bobbing logs, shoals of fish

*

Main for main
these freakish minutes
turn

    a house to a shaky boat
    with torn hatches

five foot to eight
the barometer won't play
any favourites

    if the top step shows
    you're safe

while a torch light drowns

    *

Daybreak, spirit gone
comes to reckon

    all smithereened—
    furniture, toys lie in a slop

    trees act like they've died
    but it's all in the roots (bedded,
    if the body's scraped)

    *

Heri-, hero cane,
you beat a drumskin,
sway in and jostle
as an echo
of stranger steps

some says we shouldn't be
in brackish flats

that the giver will roll and chop

*

Here to hori-zone
blues allus fall

we take our clothes and float,
slide crazy
chunks of wood

through slime

play right on—
don't, snout beaten
see another way

Banker Speak

Come roight in, take a cheer and set into 'er.
Or we might should use the pizer, unless
it's breezing up. No skeeters around.
I'll heist the window. These boxes is piled
all catawampus. Chunk that extry bottle
in the bucket, not the one with criabbs.

How you farring? I hearn you had a good cetch
last week when it was windysome.
Bee-al liketa drowned out thar, but then
he gets mommucked easy in this invairment.

Is you fixin' to go over on the Saind soid
after it gets to dark good? It was a slick cam
out there yeste'day.

We haint had much call for playing anymore.
Everything we do seems dit-dot.

I thunked up that song a while back
but the words been gone a whit now.
Leastways I could only member a smidget
when the young'uns got to askin
about Diamond Shoals. I can make like
I'm playing . . . when I clap my hands,
that's the gittar.

Did you tote the stuff over here?
I'm a gittin keerless, my shirt's begombed
with oil. All beans cooked with meat into it.
Drime, that ain't right, give me a pin
and I'll put a doast of Truth back in.

Any place else in the world is arf.

Bleeding Secrets

Slate raised from a well, Jamestown, May 2009

One way this, one way that
the grooves tell a moment
laid on a moment. What's wiped
will show at a tilt or in changing light
points of a journey. Is this a sabal palm,
a Bermuda petrel? You glimpse an island
of sweet berries, found after a faint star
flashes from shroud to shroud
in a black storm. The secretary hand
bespeaks some official (script conjoined
with doublet and slashed breeches).
Who is 'Abraham', patriarch or colonist
beside 'vial of' and 'bottle' value?
Double-loop signs may geometrize
how a stranger speaks, *chum*-my
in a mah-*kuh*-sun. On the reverse
lions rear at an angle to fleur-de-lys—
some coat of arms? A helmeted soldier
holds a woman in a ruff who stands
indignant or compliant. Other men,
one with an arrow (?) through his hat.
All in venetians, the soldier's pear-shaped.
Crypto/clear between ruled lines
a recorder states or passes a message:
| EL NEV FSH | HT LBMS | 508
| AM NON OF THE FINEST SORTE
(or MIN[I]ON OF THE FINEST SORTE).
Junked from the starving time, water
gone bad, this asks while it answers,
a grey file new in the wind's eye.

Salt Tattoo

Black blue heaves   over secret chambers
chafed coils   fever-shivers

on drench dug   waste

ding-dong   did One
muffled   hum

clang   the air today

as would   fathom
stuff from nothing

                         steepled isle
                    from a rotten butt

broke speech   to rolic burden
a swishy mass   of atoms coupled

swell-hole   switch-swathe

so this   lap-jolt
falls   to a level

in sunglaze trance   a fable inverted

might be   blood or wine

Recursive

oak
skeletons
exposed
by
a
sand
blow

*

oak
frame
and
planks

dragged
from
Atlantic
floor

langrage
cluster
bale
seals
spoons

*

unvalued
jewels
in
giddy
footing

Shell and Sheave

    I lie on my side in grains
packed   disc on pin   ever–set
beneath head and shoulder bulk
as also   its roll–twin   once all
    vibrant for tackle and rig

(double block: elm and bronze)

Salvage

Grapple this slippery hulk
in cloud-soup

      red–grey (what?)

from silt to surface
drag

    wash deep salt
    from its body,
    bathe again
    and freeze

    stiff awake

Boat Spree

Kingston-Oxford

Dim woods on either bank, a ghostly army.
Lapping water, smothered speech.
You couldn't choke Caesar off that river,
he crossed in spite of the stakes.

They awe us, these strange stars
so cold and clear. Uncaught gems
that might tell everything.

Wassermarrer?—le'ss pull on to the lock
a mile and a half above. Supposed
to have creaking gates.
The map may be right enough, if we know
whereabouts *in it* we are.

These names hide round corners
and merely peep at the stream
down one street.

There's no place for fancy stuff,
throw the lumber over. Just need
a lamp and sculls to get through
or be born on the blarmed bit
to understand.

A stiffish breeze. Always against you
whichever way you go.
Who wants to be foretold the weather?

Bearings

Make [this] . . . Inward Syon, the Syon of the ghost
Wyatt, Penitential Psalms

Silver wings catch the sun   a projectile roar

Redbrick Hilton   fenced-off future
like the lane made a turnpike

        Capability's sweep—
        meadows, tree clumps

Hard to feel back   before Brown and Adam

knots with triangular terrace,
May Lily scent

courtyard with outbuildings   pronged
from *white house*   to pepperpot lodges

grained labour of farmland, mills

        Where in heritage space
        garden-centred or grand-staired

        is the star-point you might fathom
        with splayed arms

        three foot down

Under the mound or garage block?

To see exact you must tread through years

        Hariot's waterworks plan
        with his own privy

        and elsewhere scattered
        his diagrams of house & grounds

These have a plot to the north, at the end
of a rectangular garden

        features matched (with a 3-D dwelling)
        on Treswell's plan and Glover's map

I am led down a tunnel to a little courtyard
facing the Muniment or Evidence Room
that seems too far

    Rather I'd place the site   just outside
                     the laundry cottages

This hinges on alignment
with the main house—the northeast
of that hollow square

    One may piece together   Chamber
                       Study
                       Dining room
                       Pantry
                       Kitchen

    from a sketch of door openings

Then add hubs of experiment from Hariot's will

      so to summon
    in dust & stone
  an absent voice

Exile Heart

And the withy shall be the very first tree
to perish at the heart

       Harp hung
          from
             wand or rod

               stream bubbling
                out of
                   sight

                    song
                      barely
                        callable

                            by free
                        thought
                 in lordly space

                  the Lion gate
               all lace, embroidery
            (Walpole said)

             must grub up
         roots to remake
      a world

Auger Note

Water
          bluish cool   to brownish warm
                    roiling/still/effusive

               by etch   or absent play

                    glosses
                              settlement

Hariot's source   marked on Glover's map

          Conduit head . . . Conduit fields . . .
          Waste Water

runs south-east from over the Loop
          (all grassland with trees till 1920)

     beside & across the London road

                    towards Syon House

but the whole territory is shaped by streams

     the Thames, the Brent and the Crane
     a squiggly E
     with conduit (almost) the central bar

and a misfit stream in the park

               marked by Brown's sluglike lakes

     course of a braided (ancient) Thames

leaves the abbey site   at root   a lozenge-eyot

▷

This clear again from Glover

with said channel   running in a curve

from   (the present)   Snowy Fielder Waye

down the edge of Ferney Meade, Sion Orchard

and into the Brent near its outflow to the Thames

      where *Old England*   a moth-shaped meadow

cues

        flint and stone axes, a horn,
       bronze rings, razors, swords

          found along the Reach

     in a mass

     to argue some rite

Feed/clean/transform

    a means at base

Uiscelworth   (water village)

Proximate

If as the records have it Pocahontas came
to Brentford End—lodged autumn through winter
in that last year—which house offered rest
and hope of health?

               Syon Park House
on London Road, demolished 1953. Listed
as Syon Place in 1850. Formerly
Syon House Academy, where Shelley gazed
at clouds and swallows through lofty windows,
blew up the lid of his desk and the boundary palings.

Dr Greenlaw—Scottish divine—destroyed
carved mantelpieces and kept his pupils in line
with bread skimmed sky-blue.
All classics, arithmetic, plus a dose
of geography and astronomy.

            It stood opposite the lane
leading to Syon House: so a fair candidate
for her dwelling, close to the Percy household
but private. Rolfe, tobacco farmer, may have
shared a pipe with Hariot.

But this building (brick) isn't on the Treswell plan
or on Glover's map, of the time.

Instead, on the right (North) side of the road
there's a house owned by *S*^r *Thomas Savadge*
having two red roofs—perhaps the precursor
on this same plot.

           Now the site
of a postal sorting office, in collapsed logic
some way in touch with Other worlds.

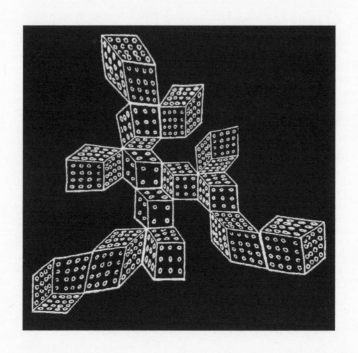

Bust Returned

There is a certaine kinde of compound called Laudanum,
which may be had at Dr. Turners, appothecary, in
Bishopgate Streate; the virtue of it is verry soveraigne
to mitigate anie payne; it will for a tyme lay a man
in a sweete trans, as Dr. Parry told me he tryed in a
fever, and his sister Mrs. Turner in hir childbirth.
John Manningham, *Diary* (1602)

Half the lively figure, blitz-filched, is back

    a ruffed and bearded Doctor
    hands clasped in prayer

        Paracelsian
        for whom a disease
        (say, a canker)
        is cured by its like—
        properties loosed
        by fire

    as the sanguine doublet may hint

Lost in someone's cupboard or attic
for seventy years
after a chancer struck

    by whatever track
    comes to rejoin
    his herbalist father

        along with Pepys & wife
        (the naval thread)

    behind spikes, skulls and crossbones,
    Saint Ghastly Grin

    church in a cluster of churches

▷

Down remote space with a plague amulet
he visits Ralegh in the Tower

has Hariot watch the sky from his roof
in *litle St Ellens, seeing but one moon*
and offers treatment

    before the rod passes

        in chemic soothe
        of belief

        oval ooze

        poplar, red mercury

to skin-build another few years

        *

Garden hush amid dane-din, herbs
beneath railway shriek stealing sun
from Gogmagog graters

    Sydon, Sything, Seething Lane—
    crossed friars, ship-goods,
    wine and parmazan

what relief comes through, cored
in traffic

a gold scallop with grooves
shielding the head, stayed and mobile

a braided gown, probative for who
will congregate

St Olave, Hart Street, 2011

Chamberscape

Maybe it's the wrong ■■■■■ we mouth up to
these pleats of sky, wanting Evidence for what
makes that thumbprint of light on the wall, the
thing back there or maybe forward skin to skin
where ■■■ is a minge sniff and all is ventrous
down dedalian conduits. Coal, wine and rough
sleep under Adelphi arches where the river no
longer presses ■■■■ whose street whose lane
over cellars strung with stalactites. Did one say
fever struck for'n-er, grapnel fingers set to haul
an alphabet through, pars-pord ■■■■ nec-rop
crush ■■■■■■ at control centre. Don't come a
knockin' when Durham House goes Algonquin
as aisley science looks for a join. The potion got
in a groined vault gives view ■■■■■■■ from
a garret over Surrey hills. This watch-birth tab
■■■■■■■■■ draws one figure over another
pulsing the memorist ■■■ world within world.

Crystal Lattice

He came out of the Clifton—doors, windows
boarded up. The piano is dead, the stone
is worth more than conversation. Oak panels,
mirrors trashed. Bertie's silhouette swings,
scent of Lillie in the wind. Non dom angles
for another use.

Photos of my uncle and cousin, June 1954,
when they lived on the corner of St John's Wood
and Edgware Road. A local for my father too,
across from Abbey Road. If I came trailing
I can't remember, but Patrick, age seven,
has his nose in a book, Brownie 'box' on the table.

In the back garden—shrubs, a barrel, tubular chairs,
umbrella-arc over pint glasses. Out front a long view
past 90, 92 and 94, all Mrs Reynall's, at least
by the late Fifties. Just one car parked in the distance.

The pub is cross-hatched for perspective,
a future drawing. Mania to quantify
like that other Harriot. *Nature is mechanical*
but then it is not seen that mechanics
contain that which is beyond mechanics.
A building, a person, a tree resolve into figures.

Stuff in the frame lies ready to rouse.
Joe tells a joke, plays a stringish piece, solo—
Forties through Sixties, well navigated.

Will it resurrect? Something zigzags
through a pinboard.

Stonehold

To live, not exist, that's the point
in Blake's quarter

> map site of working small
> in cloth or wood

a bar-crossed creature
to throw definition

> a tobacco-stained mermaid,
> carbonara twists

But hungrily the tunnel drives east,
rents soar, chains
brand any patch the same

> give us even
> a Pyrex cup
> of coffee
>
> over brew options
> to sip and go

Gastro-gent-riffs beggar the glowy maze
with wiped relation, brain broken
from hand

> as jingled app
> summons
> in-come spirit

Can't stop this luggs-uriel sweep
(designer hoodies for porn, red carpet suites)

till another rank displaces
by spin spill law

Metroconda

Cross-blade whirring head
of giant worm, a toothed wheel
throwing back spoil

Phyllis, Ada—
twins
working
from Royal Oak portal

find gnawed bison bones
in the old Westbourne

fast water
between
ice eras

grassland and forest

then on through tangled rod and gut—
sewers, power lines, foundations

even the eye of the needle, between Northern Line
and escalator tunnel

find beneath the smashed Astoria
glass sauce bottle stoppers
marmalade jars

both bores skirting Denmark Street

to the Plague Pit (No Man's Land), 13 skeletons
out of 50,000 laid in three years
under Charterhouse Square

pressure-sensored to veer correct
push off last ring

for the next advance

▷

in slow-budged clay

poison to plough
but mouldworthy, waterproof

a blue-green thread

quiet
under madness

bides the roll
of new traffic

Red Desert

Big Ben, the river, embankment
half-blanked out—abstract
blotches. You breathe
indoors, brake dust and diesel
lidded by what they call
a perfect storm.

It's not Shanghai, it's not Beijing
but something's painted
the street. It tickles your throat,
tastes metallic.

We're martians in Africa, find
by dot-dash buzzes, leave
grey fruit in a barrow.
Today lurches: the paper falls
from wall to pavement
at just the point you step.
Starlings fly another route.

What's that? Soprano shivers
someone's lost orbit. Drone
of a bell, a horn, or is it a scream?
Aummm, wye-nnn, the crave
to go over.

Any story comes in jagged pieces
with the heart outside.
Earth ferments to say a kiss
won't cure it.

Our trees are pipes and girders,
a ship sails through the park.

Chronovent

Enter a wormhole, with lightspeed
slowing time

        the shortest way
    despite shockfronts

           total blackness
      with stars extinguished
      until you arrive

           a burnhole
        in silk, a disc
        barred and cross-barred

    wanton silver

    if it isn't out there, it might be
  our inner surface

  a river-alley
wrapped in a coat
two see back to back

Stereo–isomeric

Bottle comrade, what a crow's croak
you venture, as a Tudor rose frames mine.
Who is English, a lion roars in the Tower,
grhhr, gurrh, fusky music tearing
off stone. So jars and tins sing
for an absent mate.

Your gown is my skin. This sunburn
you purchased over the main
shot convulsive through foam
to find grapes and cedars. I followed back
to make good, stayed to plant in reverse
a sort of twisted wire.

Brought the thing out of its frame
letting my fingers go. Collied, luned
your creature could climb a ladder
to dangle marks on a napkin
or think a friend into being
as island sol strobes into island fog.

We step down the Strand by doorways
that hide great gardens. A rush of figures
see nothing, no master face, no mimic grin.
Any seeker off the plain table fades
from the record and waits for another
to crossruff space.

2

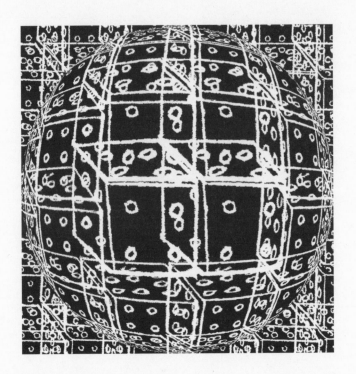

Saxicave

Nunhead bones. A vault removed
from the Old Lady. Under leaping fire
and walls remade. Nothing stops
the course of gold.

To sweep by permit of heaven:
spice smoke and a rattle
like chariot wheels on stone.

Houbledon, first Governor,
jaw clamped against swart riot,
grabs the church—propped Wren Gothic
in second ruin—
to build a flank of leverage.

Would you garden here
with a bright copper shovel
when the Picquet's on guard?

Stay traveller, lightly tread:
here lies a star/digit plotter
who probed, the Nose of England
from Oxford to Virginia
to Syon on Thames.
Leaving does not shut
the story of his days.

Corpse Candle

I will & bequeath unto the Earle
One woodden Boxe full or neere full
of drawne Mappes standing nowe
at the Northeast windowe of that Roome
wch is Called the parlor
of my house in Syon.

I give unto the aforesaid Earle
my two pspective trunckes
wherewth I use espeatially to see
Venus horned like the Moone
and the Spotts in the Sonne.

I give unto my servaunte Christopher Tooke
the residue of my Cases of pspective trunckes
wth the other glasses of his owne making
(excepting two great longe trunckes
Consisting of many partes wch I give
unto the said Earle of Northumberland
to remayne in his Library for such uses
as they may be put unto).

Concerninge my debts, I doe acknowledg
that at this psente I owe moneyes
to Monseir Mayornes a Potycarie,
to my Brewer dwelling at Braynford end
& to Mr John Bill Staconer for Bookes.

I ordayne and Constitute Nathaniell Thorperley
first to be Overseer of my Mathematicall Writinges
to be received of my Executors
to peruse and order and to separate
the Cheife of them from my waste papers,
to the end that after hee doth understande them
hee may make use in penninge such doctrine
that belonges unto them for publique uses.

Item: divers waste papers (of wch some
are in a Canvas bagge)

of my Accompts to Sr Walter Rawley
for all wch I have discharges or acquitances
Lying in some boxes or other
my desire is that they may bee all burnte.
Alsoe there is an other Canvas bagge
of papers concerning Irishe Accompts
(the psons whome they Concerne are dead
many yeares since in the raigne of queene Elizabeth)
wch I desire alsoe may be burnte
as likewise many Idle paps & Cancelled Deedes
wch are good for noe use.

Aryott

there be two maner of herryottes . . .
Fitzherbert, *Boke of Surveyeng*

One or other the lord will get you/best live beast
or chattel/takes like sword or armour/
a horse, a feather-bed/print of what
was warm

heregeatu heregeatwe

the market bit, as if in castle-frame a villain
were free

> to answer in gold
> the trumpet

> raw dirt scraped off
> drains and pipes

> some halfling
> presence

cold and wet where no bars are flashing
(not any, like song this July)

slumped/removed
for translation

boated (it might be)
to last exchange

Ozaena

No cure for this grief. Inject water
and lay to the sores either double clouts
or lint moystned in this water
as you shall think fit morning and evening.

Shun all meats which are of an hard concoction
or afford a corrupt and evill juyce.
Like those Indians which are sober
in their eatinge and trinkinge
and doe not oppress nature
by unseasonable banketts.

A dream of navigation. Great spouts
as though heaven and earth should meet.
A silent scream as Cardes, Bookes, writings
the sailors cast over boord.

Old venturers hang together,
Thomas with Thomas. Past all stains
of travel, learning has a body absolute.
Threadneedle street: Buckner's house,
sea–marke of utmost saile.

A gleam of wrestling fire
sinks out of sight, retreats
to the chancell Quire,
St Christopher le Stock.

Runagate

No Star-chamber but a great blasing-star
the only subject almost of discourse.

An angry star, reddish with a long tail
and ever there. A letter such as none
can translate. Keepe rash imaginations
till you sleepe.

Queen Anna still at Denmark House
awaits burial.

Billiard balls, how they roll and collide.
Lord Percy's passion. As below, so above.

Notes fleshed on reflexion
of bodies, dash and pull
in a diagram. Motions
compounded. Who understands this
is master of other cases and the whole.

Solution and results. The logic
can wait.

Majesties or Mates

I beseeche your Ladyshep that you will . . . intreat [Sir
Thomas Wilson] to surcease the pursuit of my hosbans
bookes or lybrary: they being all the land and lyveing
which he left his poore child

   Lady Ralegh to Lady Carew, 8 November 1618

To whose apprentise intellegans
would you send
these leaves amassed? that one
may march or sayle
through ages past, plod long
but loosely take
the knot or pith that makes
this present.

A *Wagg* sholde not meete
Wood or *Weed*
for timber will rot and frett
the halter.

The booke is a being that does not
cum singell: has markes of the user
like a pointing hand, stans with fellowes
to forme a World.

This Spenser is stabbed for sewing,
has *Despair* in the margin, yet goes proud
with Belphebe's promise. This Strabo,
this Copernicus, this Paracelsus,
this America in three partes, this treatis
of specters, this Augustine—have ther classe
high or low, reachable to inquire & joine.

As a head imbalmed that store remaines.

Command Performance

What closest friend comes back in chains.
No gold, no sonne,
onlie a wall to address *if* over *if.*
(Yt is thought Sir Walter shall pay
this new reckoning upon the old score.)
. . . .

Two fits of an agew.
Thankes to god.
of calling god to witness.
note/That He speake justly & truely.
~~Touchinge his~~
    that
1).   Concerning his loyalty to the King
2).   of slanderous speeches touching
     his ma^{ty}.
6).   Sr L. St[ukely]: A letter on London hy way.
          10,000^{li}
           no such proffer
7).   Mine of Guiana
     a wilfull fellow crossd.
8).   Came back by constreynt.
10). Company used ill in the voyadge.
11). Spotting of his face & conter-
         fetting sicknes
12). The E. of Essex.

Come not to feare or flatter
now ye subject of Death.

Lastly. he desired the company
   to joine with him in prayer. &c.

Some found fault that his face was west-ward
and wold have him turned
whereupon rising he saide yt was no matter

▷

which way a mans head stoode
so his heart lay right.

Two blowes to sever
what is kept for his lady
in a red velvet [leather?] bagg.

Venom to Balm

Ingrate inflate—knot of Mouth or Table friends

will not say they got meanes to build
for all the clay in Kilburne

       slink away as the Thames
leaves dungie slime

       change their shirtes as the moone
without washing-balls make sweete

       offer summes by bond or bill
that split like bummes with phantom fruite

       telle of Law when one
would stand upon fact.

A deal comes out of a deale so the snake
eates the toade and the toade the snaile

              This my *negrum* inke would prove,
              pen-neb turning to fork.

Fate-borne-Dogs-to-Barke will flie
upon those who try New Worldes
even where hony-hearted wine powres forth.

An O without a figure makes the foole
who treads the bows of Lundun

       (windinge banks or arches)

You may argue the tosse, changing one scheme
for an Other, limping by the New Exchange
to saile for Cork & that broad Orenoke

till Nothing brings you all thinges

Akontant (Playster)

                    I
                  would
                  watch
                  and
                  not
                    be
                     an
                  object
                    of
                  gaze

muttusk
mocosiit

                    I
        can   skip
        nod   over
        curtsy   field
        clasp   wood
        hands   wheel
          kiss   bare

        golden   give
        weed   coal
        you   clouds
        take   weeping
        from   weather
        us   lungs

        trick'd up   O little
        chest afire   *Thomas*
        it goes sore   from here
        to return   by spout
        of bigger   streams
    with bells & beads our neech or meteor

Travice

Princesse from the womb of a taverne
silent (though she hath our tongue & dress)
till I venture Virginian speche.

To be a little out of the smoak of the citie
they (Mr Rolfe and she) are come to Brainford.

She that was Matoaka or Pokahuntas (Little-wanton)
is by baptism the Lady Rebecka.

He says his hartie and best thoughts
were intangled in a laborinth
so he was awearied to unwinde his selfe thereout.
And the gayning of a soule removes anie blot
of impurity. (This plea made publique.)

She, the very Nonparall of that kingdome,
is of countenance & proportion moste pleasing
and possessd of wit & spirit. Her hair darke
and skinne dyed tawnye, as is ther custome.

She weares now a lace whisk & copataine
and will goe to Court, with her father counsaillor,
to witnesse a Maske at the banketting house.

This Tomocomo did set up with notches on a stick
the numbers of men he saw from Plimmouth
to London, but his arithmetike soon failed.

To morrow they shal across the waye to Syon
& there meete her Ladyship. My Lord in the Towre
may mende Pokahuntas muscle-shel earringes.
I would question her of ore and finde a path back
in wordes.

There is that in her I shall not knowe.

Succotash

A man melancholy. In yeares about sixty.
First broughte the use of that Virginia smoak.
An ulcer in the left nostrell eats up
the septum of his nose, holds the lips
hard and turned upwards.
It has crept well into the nose.
Calamitous pain.

Part falls off, leaves the flesh healthy.
The crack also disappeares.

Let us drive on in earnest by this arte
ordained, most illustrious Sir.
The worldes glory passes away.
Every thing will pass away.
We shall pass, you will pass, they will pass.

Part of that callous matter still remaines
near the top and in the angle
but the laterall parts are in condition.
A good and healthy pus exudes,
sometimes more sometimes less.

Apply red mercury precipitate,
some oyntment of poplar.

Pills. Catalogues. Perkes.

Baseless Fabrick

And yet evin amonges suche sciences, those had
in most price [are they] that draw nearest to . . .
Folie. For . . . Mathematicall professours blowe
theyr nayles: Astronomers are laught to scorne:
Sophistrers are naught set by: Onely a Phisicion (as
Homer saieth) *is more worth than twentie of the rest.*
Yea and commenly the rassher, the uncunnynger,
and lesse circumspect the undertaker of any of
those usuall sciences is, the more yet is he regarded
and allowed evin amonges great men also.

Erasmus, *The Praise of Folie*, tr. Chaloner

```
                Hee
            is   parted
        no              on
      thing            sayl
      where            wingd
      cheape           shipp
      mans               in
      humor          setting
      does              sun
        not          finds
            availe
```

carne vale   *currus navalis*

Deaths fool   Boggon at
limber-hole   runs & flies

air-looped token
to credit or discount

wheel spoke
figure
the thing
it self

Some See, Some Doe Not

```
F                     HIGH-WAVED
A                         E
R                         A
R                         DREAR
E                         I
F                         V
E                         E
T                         RECKON
C                             E
H                             V
T                             E
A                     RIGHTER
N                         O
D                         U
A                         N
S                     WRIED
I                         H
T                         E
W                 WHIPSAWN
E                     R
R                     O
E                     N
B                     GOES
E                         H
Y                         E
O
N                     TOP-ON-TOP
D                    TRADUCTION
S                  ALL-LANGUAG'D
E                  TO PITCHY
A                     PLAGUE-SHAFT
M
A             YOU SUCH ANOTHER
N                 IN LABOUR TRYED
N                    AS HEAVENS
E                   LIGHTS
R          ARE LONG
```

Briny Shifts

. . . no conference had with any one living in all the novelties
I presume I have found. Only some one or two places I have
shewed to my worthy and most learned friend, M. Harriotts,
for his censure how much mine owne weighed.

> Chapman, Preface to the Reader,
> *The Whole Works of Homer*

Yet Homer *being my roote I can not die.*
> Chapman, To *Mr Harriots*, accompanying *Achilles Shield*

Take your free way: onely this must be perform'd
before you stere your course for home: you must
the way to Pluto overcome and sterne Persephone,
to forme your passe by the dark-browd prophet
whose soule can clearly and firmely see.
Dig (of a cubit every way) a pit, and powre in it
a solemne sacrifice. For which, take honey & wine
with water, and adde to these the whitest flowre.
Then vow to all the weake necks of the dead
that, treading the Ithacensian shore, thou shalt burn
thy most-esteemed goods in deare blood. But here
draw thy sword, stande firme, nor suffer one
of all the faint shades of the dead to approch
till thou hast heard their king, the wise Tiresias,
who will tell the measure of thy way
by fishe-strewne seas. Make diametric passage,
where cloud obscures outright, to that shore
where growe tall firres and sallowes,
that thou may finde the powres beneath, and learn
a doome that is not straight. Take counsaile
betwixt the prease of shadowes, that thou see again
thy Countrey and thy Queene. Walk out from where
heroes wives and daughters lead their second lives
about the blacke blood throngd, in show
of times before, to plow the broad seas billowes.

Harbourage

What does a man neede with ripe river aire?

One hogshead of beare from Braynford, a rynlet
of old Clarett, a pottell of mallmesye, a pynt
of ynnke, pennes, five quyer of Rochel paper,
a pound of pynnedust, wex lights, a fire forke,
three perspective Cylinders, a glasse of oyll,
streyners, wild tansy & dasye rotes, wormeseed,
a box of codynoke, tothe pikes, tobacco & pipes,
ij paier of neytherstocks, ij Kilkenny ruggs, a chaire
with greene cloth, hanginges of forrest worke
with halfe moones, one lardge mapp of the world.

Great warres and no blows. Here ought I
try farther this frame celeste, like Homer's face
laced with a triangle. What black springes
lye beyond cut stone, goe beneathe a white cube
with reaching limbs. Some eternesse
maybe bides through doores and staires,
a spirite that would have you look, with markes
not grudged at or slubberd up with felowshippe.

These riches knowe their proper stint, that both
possessyon and diversyon make a searchinge eie
scan the utmost bound. Through mucke-pits
even a jewell house is formed: such knowledge
lastinge over tyme and date. Or solides brought
from dissolution. So runnes my course a while still.

Pallatyne Knot

The ladye Dorothy at Essex house
for the river showe: fiery balls in the ayre,
floting castles. Then to White-hall
(against my lord's will, for Tongues
shall clatter). Her mother sayes
she must goe forth, gallant,
to the Banketting-house
this Valentines day.

As a parcell of these nuptialls
is to be performd that play or Maske, *The Tempest*
by Mr Shakespeare

wch shall fill a peece of greene cloth
and resound the *Companie*.

The Earle would have me watch.

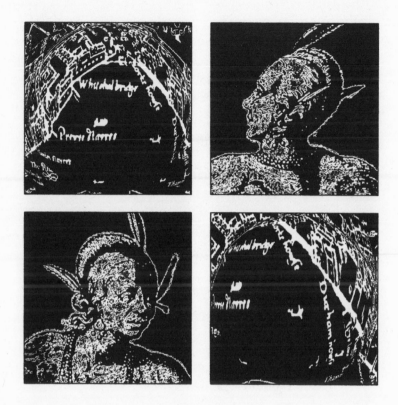

Sciography

Mr Percy returnd from Virginia
hath Money owinge
to Cap Lawson & James Mower
wch shal be settled

speakes of the Tyme of hunger
when some did eate Bootes, unknowne Rootes
& deade corpes dugge outt of graves,
one killing his verie wyfe for foode

a Sequell to that Salvage spectacle
we saw aboute Munster

Nothinge holds one state from another
but a certayne array as forces
in this parcel of partes

He composes letters
into night (a selfe in reach),
occupies his olde chamber
with feather bedd & boulster

hath ever that love of riche apparrell,
as Incarnadyne Velvett
(he sayd, for the Indian chiefe)

waits to make triall
whether his fitts here in England
shal be more greevous
than he felt them in other partes
neerer the lyne

Things Unspoke

If the spottes   if they

    come   and goe

     shifting

     shade/station

              that *aliens*

         the kingly

       gold

                   puts out

                 the nice face

             that's set

         to sustain

but we knowe

      the tissue's

        penetrable

        (as a new starre

            in *Cassiopeia*)

     so   in manshape

    the fleshbeam

won't   turn steadie

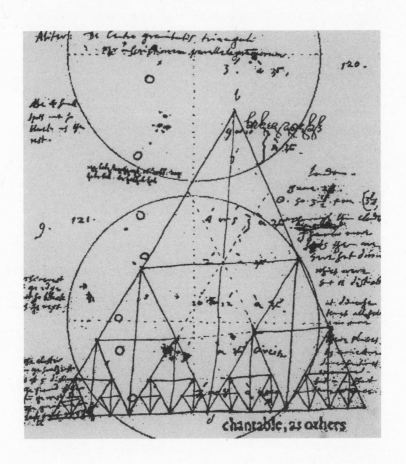

Spotted Body

It being a frost and a mist I saw the sonne
twise or thrise, once with the right ey
and other time with the left.

In halfe an houre space I saw three blacke spots.
The greatest, somewhat ragged, was most oriental
and of apparent angle about 2´. The other two
were nere of one bignes: 1´ magnitude,
or there aboutes.

After this the sonne was too cleare.
To see what lies there or shiftes you may profitt
from thick ayer, thin white cloudes or mist.

Another daye they were eight in all.
The cluster of 4 orientall are the one great spot
which appeared before. That under the center,
with that at the top, were seen also before.
The two most occidental we saw not before.
The three occidental nere the limbe
seeme not so darke as those oriental.
Sir Wm Lower & Christopher saw them with me
in several trunckes.

Next daye I saw the great spots or cluster of 4
twise in a short time through a thinne rag of a cloud,
the cloudes quickly obscuring the Sonne.

At 12^h all the sky being cleare and the Sonne,
I saw the great spot but no more.
My sight was after dim for an houre.

I observed thorough the thick ayer
and also through my coloured glasses
but saw no more: it seemed to me
that a greate glasse wold make them appeare
devided or more different.

▷

I noted the southern 3 lye
almost parallel to the ecliptick
when they were not soe yesterday.

I saw the same as the day before
but with some difference:
one semed fayer & great
and seen alone with the smaller instrument,
one more westerly, dim yet certayne
and an other smal one easterly & close by.

They generally seem bigger
being niere the middle than the sides.

15 spots in all. The four on the west limb
not so black as they were before.

3 spots. That nerest the limb long and dim,
crooked & narrower than I have noted.

Blacke to grey, grey to black
over days & months—the patterne
seene difficultely.

Undernote (Somnium)

In my Dreame there are as many problems as lines.
Some have to be solved by sight and symbols,
others by what is mouthed. People want pastymes
that will not wrinkle their brow
but to explain the Moone your storie needs
a reason added to a reason.

We must have the freedom to invent
as a character written backwards.

An old joke goes, I'll believe it
rather than go into the matter myself.
So: by *what is said of what is said*
we fore-trace patternes.

Glint. Witness. Essaie.
If philosophers lie in wait with ladders
they scoop out stuffe beyond.

The full moone rising and climbing over houses
seems equal to the rim of a keg: when it mounts
to mid-heaven it hardly matches the width
of the human face.

How does our globe appeere from there?
A bloudy platter, muddy football, silver pin-pricke
in the void, or dim fire. Some moment
is the figure of Ocean, then it's a little Continent
hammered.

A dozing draft gets you into the middle air,
hurled as if by gunne-powder. You float
in vast black silence then drop with a thud
to the surface. You wake weary
on charcoal dust in a white dawn.

Puffs of vapour, a plain with chinkes
and gulfes, a giddy bridge over tumbled rock.

▷

I did read so much in Plutarch. Onely this I can add:
There is Subvolva and Privolva, the part with sight
of our Earth and that deprived of it.
One hemisphere is like our towns and gardens,
the other like forests and deserts.

The creatures growe to great size but perish quickly.
They move as reptiles across ramparts,
shed skin in a hollow when the husk is roasted.

* * * * *

Wind and the rattle of rain wipe what's left.
Returning, I find my head covered with a pillow
and my body with blankets.

Johannes Kepler

Cubic Triolet

not everie part seene
tells its place in here,
spot in life betweene
not everie part seene
spells space to mean
as a bore in a sphere,
not everie part seene
tells its place in here.

Archemaster

Do you not startle, to see every day
inventions taken from you?

      It comes into my fantasy
      to write a boke   stagger
                  I   try
          in the ocean of space   ever
                              for
                    reasons

      one speck which describes   d
      another   a
                          n
      but . . . figures in columns   c
                          e

    I wait for the whole
    to manifest while others
    show their proofs

a tainted lord, a tainted house
limit ventures
on this paper-sea
            where reputation
            a gilded cup
            may sink

Numbers I would not willingly cloake
go absent/to the next stage
you move

      a mole in inky depths
      just here
      by lamp-shine

Mariners Mirror

Magnify first by 6 with a Dutch Spyglass:
the moon over the Thames
is a ball with a curved seam.
Over this verge, a little ragged, are seas
I'll hatch or score: ye *Caspian*, great rug-fleck,
then below, *Foecund* and *Tranquill*
a jointed arm with tiny ears,
and either side
a dream cup and nectar scutch.

The whole brimme along shewes coasts
like a booke of voyages, the matter we know
obliquid, unsettled. What shifts or crumbles
in this continent we must bear in the mean.
Some partes montenous, others like valleys
in shadow. That which I specially observed
was a promontory in the body of the feyned man.
I could not set down the figure of all
but by memory because I was troubled
by the reume. Montaynous with an opening
in the middest & some black passage
from it to the man in the moone.

In the full she appeares
like a tarte, here a vaine of bright stuff,
there of darke, and so confusedlie
al over, that without a truncke
to point up from my garret
I see nothing notable.

Thomas Hariotus
oho trahit mutas
said to unbelieve.

By this tube
the point of quadrature seek
nomo, mono, noom
nus, uns
erath, hater, reath

▷

per stellas clock or watch—
$9^h.46'$: not yet a right line but almost.
$10^h.52'$: a right line, an accidental rag or two
at & nere the lower corner being obstructed.
$11^h.30'$: yet continuing. Others say
wanting.

Looke the obser[vation] papers—
first takes in crayon. As palisade craters,
ink to record what traverse

a pencil stare into sharper grip
for any translated spirit.

1610

Sept.b. 10

D. hor. 7½.

3 days old

hor: 12

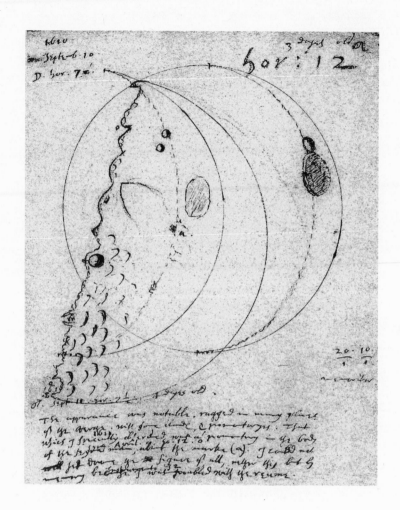

20. 10.

1610

Sept. 11. hor. 7¼. 4 days old.

The appearance was notable, rugged in many places
of the border, will some shade & promontoryes. That
which I principally discribed, was ye promontory in ye body
of the [illegible] about the marke (a). I could not
[illegible] set downe ye figure of all, when the last &
[illegible] bright promontoryes was troubled with ye veume.

Scope

Reeling notes in a tube, not that
forwarde and backwarde whirl, an orbes
quire, but spots marked
by ground and polishd glasse
in a thinkable rounde: the held picture
you read at twenty miles
or so many semidiameters of the Earth.

We had from Netherland these instruments
that we make also in several sortes
with bulge and hollow
at either ende, one fitted for the eye.

It is an engine to catch starres
as the *Iliade* in a wall-nut shell
comes manifest.

What if in that huge space there remaine
ever fixed
infinite nomber
which doe flee our sight?

A flute-case then is a tall cedar
joyned to clouds sliding at the edge.

We climb this oriel-shaft
with drum-head pulse in hard reverie,
see prospective (all on fire)

shapes beyond, silent room.

Joyned Inverse

The truth when it is seen
is knowne without other evidence.

curve of a lobbed or shot body?
Guiana?
calculation
not taken to the end

A man of wordes and not of deedes
    is like a garden full of weedes
A man of deedes and not of wordes
    is like a privifull of tourdes

Parabola

The parable being made & understoode
continued, a man may cut of from it
the species of all randons observatis observandis.

A mappe, carde or plat
does describe & measure
as the Gunner plants his shot.

So the modell of any state in Lines.
When halfe is not told us
we mark the poyntes
to engage.

Dec 24. 4. 5ᵃᵐ ½ I saw the comet ☿.☿. almost in a
right line with the 2 stars of the angle of the
beare & 13½ distant fro the top of the angle
... The angle dim & pointing
to the lowest & neerest of ♐

A B C the triangle of ...
A D B ~ A E F triangle of ...
A F B the triangle of ...
A F G triangle of ...
F G B the triangle of ...
... A F G ...
... H I ...
G H is equall to C E.

E K parallell to F B & the triangle A E K ...
...
... one line A E

Jacobopolis

Mr Warner hath a letter from Mr Percie
who names theyr towne James-fort,
which is liked best because it comes neere
to Chemes-ford.

The river, that ebbes & flowes
a hundred and threescore miles,
where ships of great burthen may harbour
in safetie, is proclaimed the Kings River.

This Fort is built triangle wise,
having three Bulwarkes at every corner
like a halfe Moone.

There have died Captaine Gosnold, with others,
of Swellings, Flixes & Burning Fevers.

But howsoever, this Countrey is a fruitfull soile.

Excursive

Her majestie here at Syon with my Ladye,
she promising to sweaten the King's displeasure.

A small consorte such as Sir R. Grenville had
in *The Tiger* did delighte us much:
that still musicke of violls, with orpharion & flute.

We have wire-string and cats-gut men,
and strong-breath'd hoboys
as before, in that sea-charged companie.
But I know not whether their endeavours were inough
to rivall a masque with paynted scenes
and fine dancing (though my Ladye
has a new bathing-house & cabinettes
which she might showe).

One at the toppe has sway, but *non plus ultra:*
there are stairs and passages not visited
even by the sun.

My Lord doth sing still and soe often one noate
that workes around the court. Absent,
he directs husbandrie, some smalle licence,
but starlings covet our vine wall, snails our gardens.
The countess tries to avoid harshe language,
wills for her children a better state.

When the blacke ox has trod on your foot
some balm may yet arrive.

I did present the Queene with a viol of water
which ebbes and flowes at the same time
as the river. We showed her the pepper-boxes
behind the White House and she sayd
she would come the backe way next time
and aske the porter for a pinch.

▷

There's grace perhaps in a farthingale
with soft pleats: the coyle will stay
any swerve or swag.

Against those who'd kill our worke,
think a charm in Blackness—
What worde is that that changeth not
though it be turned & made in twaine?

Beam Show

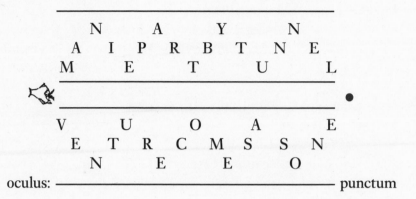

```
        N       A       Y           N
    A   I   P   R   B   T   N   E
  M       E       T       U           L
```

oculus: ——————————————————————— punctum

```
    V       U       O       A           E
      E   T   R   C   M   S   S   N
        N       E       E       O
```

passage undirect/yet the readiest
in land impassable

river of light
to riches
hidden

```
        B
        O       G
        U   N
          N I
            C
```

TRUE

TO

```
            A
        P
        P
      A
      R
        E
          N
            T
```

Trace or Traile

M[r] [Geo.] Percy
    Cap Bartholomew Gosnold   }   for
    M[r] Roger Stransom   }   Virginia

Glasse ball: to finde its burning point

Path of rays. A law of swerves?
Table to render things easy
(M[r] Kepler would have)

           Glasse prisma:
           what travels
           within—
           or not

        Light comes white
      to the charta:
    yellow edge
  (one angle)
    red edge
      (an other)

Observation not to be trusted (but with *Argus eies*)
as the right line is manie
going by partes penetrable (void)
in a body of atomes

        Veer and tacke / rayn-droppe
          splay / index to better
            cardinal / a small
              great globe
                pro-
                cess

Great Cordial

*Sir Walter Raleigh was a great Chymist . . . He studied
most in his Sea-Voyages, when he carried always a
Trunke of Bookes along with him, and had nothing to
divert him.*

Aubrey, *Brief Lives*

a skilfull and learned Chymist *can aswell by separation
of visible elements draw helpfull medicines out of poyson,
as poyson out of the most healthfull hearbs and plants
(all things having in themselves both life and death)*

Ralegh, *The History of the World*

Our rosy star: this viall having ✳✳✳✳✳✳✳✳✳✳✳✳✳✳✳✳✳
[Virginia snakeroote & Tupara] as soveraigne partes[+]
essencified, with things of different natures,
Bark of Sassafras, Aloes-wood &c.

[+] or more deep, *chinchona, coca*

The Three Magi

It's a fine tale, *Heriot, Hues & Warner*
round a table in the Tower
at the earle's chardge, so they might *converse
singly or together*, as Sir *Walter* did. These
and *Nath. Torperley*, forming *an academy*
in prison.

From charts obscure
the *Atlantes* of the Mathematic world
talk seeds, spots
at the heart of a land
where you cannot freely philosophize.

Brasen spheres and a skull cleaved
to get the working clear

       tentare, tendere—
       feel, try, tempt

       a stretch
       into
       mist

School of spirits summoned
for deepe searching
in cob-castle.

Wallis has it from Wood
who fixes it (enlarged) from Aubrey
who spins it (gossipy) from Pell and writer anon.
who gets the germ (perhaps) from Dr R[h]ead,
Hariot's last physician:
Chirurgicall Lectures of Tumors & Ulcers (1635).

If there was a *handsome table*, these men
came severally at intervals.
But truth tips (like theirs) a *gyddie platt*:

this world, its parts runne
as an old shippe that has had
all or most of her peeces changed.

On a *wardour's* trick in the yard
(nightwatch)
magick at the smallest jarre
drifts down

flames crackle, wheels whir,
lips murmur or hum

Some calculator sees his shadow's
carried a boatload of fusty books
past the face of a tapestry breathing
or found a skeleton with an howre-glass
on his Lo.'s Turkey carpet.

Sixteen years to probe, what are follies
to a *black velvet gowne laced with gold?*
None who *might* steps beyond—
you shift and return
as Hariot's *sonne dyall*
on the south wall
can declare.

Just say these fellows
are points on a board, touching
when the moment allows.
Out of a slashed nought, *north* driven
the brain yaws
to figure what's there and why.

Prison Pastymes

Towarde the makinge of a Styll house in the Towre—
viz for bricke & tyles for the furnace and harth: xij^s
for boordes & quarters to make sheilfes & Staresteps: $xxij^s$
for xv barres of yron: xij^s for ij Cestrons of lead: xv^s
for a Copper vessell and necessaries to yt: vij^s
for ij funells of platte: vij^d
for a paire of bellows: x^d for a fyre rake of yron: xij^d
for a greate padlocke and a Screne: $xiiij^d$
for a steile Chesell: $iiij^d$ a handmer & handsawe: xvj^d
for a paire of Longe Compasses: $iiij^d$
ij Rulers with plumetts: ij^s for glasses: $xxxj^s$
for viij gallons of Canarye: $xxiiij^s$ spirits of Roses: xij^s
for sugar Cenomon water & other materials: x^s ij^d
And for diverse other necessaries as Colebasketts
handbusketts Syves payles potts pannes packe threed
tape wyer Streyners treys pastbord wax paper matts
Candlesticks postage and such like: $xxij^s$ vj^d In all

	£	s	d
For an inlaide Table for the Practice of the Arte Militaire . . . . }	4	18	0
For making a Mold of Brass to cast Souldiers in & making 140 of them, with wyer for Pikes . }	2	16	8
Making 300 leaden men, &c., with a Box to put them in . . . . }	1	7	8
The Table, and Points; and gildinge the same .	3	17	6

Henrye Taylor, Clarke of his Lo. ship's kitchen, *Accomptes*

Lord in Limbo

Questions, have we enough
from a trail of gunpowder: as quho
caste the King's nativity—combust
in the ascendant, a human signe
joyn'd to the taile of the Dragon—
and if ever milorde did affirme
he would take the Catholicques part.

*Ther was a discourse
but he remembreth not particulars.*

Some jealous quipster breathes a name.
The court glowes like rotten wood
which beetles bore unseen.

How whispers make halberds.
Any spiall of purpose gives entercourse
with actors lined in a cupboard.
To dispell this scent you'd need go
to the Chilterne Hilles.

Rawleigh, 'father of wiles', is caged already.
Two roomes in the Bloody Towre
with a door open to the garden.

A barge brings Percy, shoots beneath
the arch to slipp'ry steps, *don't stride
too short into the water.* By iron tread
he's gated as a friend, behind portcullis teeth
and a rampart—that *gallery*
noisome with savour of ditches.

Next, by persuasion, Martin Towre,
over against the Mount. No river view
through window bars in thick walls.
'Boullen' carved in stone
beneath a rose. What you may learn
out of the grate.

Why Martin? At th'east ende,
a name transferred from another tower.
Bird or man who dwells aloft,
migrant to strait quarters.

The first comminge is full of passion
from wharfe to vault,
a duskish cylindre through infinite space:
the plotte which holds
a file of ancestors, a father's bones.

Your Majestie, that is soe greate a Scholler
cannot but know how impossible it is
to prove a negative.

It were fair walking on the leads. Turne
from Ordnance roofs, cannonball pyramids,
a pen of ample state, to hamlets & fields
over the moat—the Minories, East Smithfield,
greene out to Epping and Essex.

A pegg in a hole for everie span
of this pavement.

You can eyelet the breast, fitte the will
to its lodging, scan what's brittle
in baffled glory. So castell'd
a league from tottering favor,
you may this lot inlarge, chyl-cold
to extirpe anie care.

Remember, Remember

A rider with a red beard
from the North (a lie)

    dust in the courtyard

    conference aside
    (*sawsed mee with a Gudgeon*)

    then to dinner
    with company enough

Lower, Hariot, Torperley
spoke of the stars & channels

Captain Whitlocke, the young Lord
fooled with spoons

Cosin Thomas, casually here
asked *what newes of the parlemente?*
(a bayte to discover
what matter has seeped)

    he not collecting rents
    but under this noble name
    leasing a cellar
    for fuel

we may not know what we know
(*best witchcraft is Geometrie*)

lines cut crosswise
make their match angles equal
and the go-on says
reasons fit, *of which of whether*

    a pumpkin slit
    is a forked flash

Syon, the fourth of November last,
smudged dots between two half-circles:
to have been there is enough,
a body stuffed in a bottle
with the cork rammed home

Seal up *Master Herriotts studie door & chests*

To fling a figure of a king's life
makes he (the doer) *a funeral beaste*

Kin Cuts

At night was there a sumptuous shew presented by ye Q.
and some dozen Ladyes all paynted like Blackamores
face and neck bare and for ye rest strangely attired in
Barbaresque mantells to ye halfe legge, having buskins
all to be sett wth jewells, wch a wave of ye sea as it weare
very artificially made and brought to ye stage by secrett
ingines cast forth of a skallop shell to performe ye residue
of ye devise of dansing etc. The *personators* of these acts
weare hard to be knowne. In the cuming owt, a banquet
wch was prepared for the K. in the great chamber was
overturned table and all before it was skarce touched.
It weare infinit to tell you what losses there weare of
chaynes, Jewells, purces, and such like loose ware. And
one woeman amongst the rest lost her honesty, for w^ch
she was carried to the porters lodge being surprised at
her business on the top of the Taras.

––––––––––

The women kinde in this Countrey doth pounce and race
their bodies, legges, thighes, armes and faces wth a sharpe
Iron, wch makes a stamp in curious knots, and drawes the
proportion of Fowles, Fish or Beasts, then wth paintings
of sundry lively colours, they rub it into the stampe w^ch
will never be taken away, because it is dried into the flesh
where it is sered. Serpentes are wrought wth blacke spots.
In each eare commonly they have 3 great holes, whereat
they hang bracelets or chaines. They weare a chaine of
pearles, or beades of copper, or smoothe bones 5 or 6 fold
obout their necks. They tye deers skinne doubled about
them crochinge hygher about their breasts wch hange
down before almost to their knees, and are almost naked
behinde. For the cut of their haire: maids grate their
heads all but the hinder part, but the wives weare it all
of a length. This performed wth 2 shels.

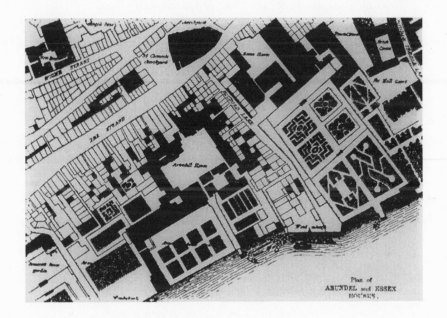

Plan of
ARUNDEL and ESSEX
HOUSES.

Thames Scull-impique

A note of rewardes geven the last progress
to the sixt of Septembre:

geven by Myles to ij watermen that brought the cannowe to my Lords howse	v	s
geven by my Lord to the Virginian	iiij	s
geven to my Lord of Northumberlandes man that brought grapes	v	s
geven by *Sir* Walter Cope to the keeper of the Hous	x	s
geven to the Virginians	v	s
geven to a payre of ores that waited on the Virginians when they rowed with ther Cannow	xij	d

Accomptes, Cicill Hse [1603]

the season of the sommer being so farre spent
we are gotten safe
with no plaguie carkas
from the stayres to the Strond

a wonder in these queasie times

tre-trowe & scoopes their use
here acted, that else
hang from a cabinet ceiling
but halfe salsipotent

a pithie shewe for oure disport—
glode on the glassie streame
by course exacte

this salvadge craft
clapped agayne

through gardens, bricke and tymber

Back Current

Captayne Mace his pinnes returned
not fynding those people
wch were lefte

extremitie of weather
& losse of some principall
ground–tackle

Sr Walter Ralegh to Weimouth.
Askes by righte of patent
that this other cargoe (of Cap Gilbert)
wch is without leve
be confiscate

Sassafras come to London in carte.
remember to arest.
Mr Willis book, Bacon.
Tiling any hose.
coniunctium solis et lunae.

A horse for Kit
A ribbon for my dagger
Tobacco
Pipes

Mace Memoranda

for the sufficient Mariner, S.M.—
his viadge out of Weimouth:

Whether compasses or diales.
Copper not brasse 20 or 30 pound in plates.
  some as thin as paper and small and great.

Hatchetes. 5. doz.	Mattockes. 20
Knives. 50. doz.	Iron shovelles 20.
lead and powder.	Sheres.
powder and shot.	Sawes.
clothes for men.	
Booke of voyages.	

What is this.   Kecow hit tamen.*   What is your name.

January .29 ♀ .   1601
                                —
                                1602

Copper in plates.   32li
delyfer theym
at 16d the pound. } + 42s + 8d
276 pieces.   }

a payne of glass   } +   3s + 4d
and punches—   }   _____

                        46s + 0d
videlicet.
of 7 inches, square.   10.
          round.   05.
6 inches. square.   20.
          round.   10.
4 inches. square   40.
          round.   20.
3 inches. square   100.
of a smaller
size and iblonge   }   71.
and different begnesses. }

                              __
                              276

* *kaquew hettamun*

Prime Runne

All things to be resolved againe into Water (Thales)

This flow, how to move it better,
with mendinge of Condeyth pipes
& tylinge the Cestern Chamber

   First, the lye of troughes & Channelles

      From the Springhead
      to the house of S^{ir} F Darcy
      I thinck

     to the farmes, the pond
     (where is a cesswell
     for empying ye pipes)

    another to the Stables
    and still another
    to the Laundry & Privy T.H.

  Then a junction at the House
  serving 2 cellar drains

   a Cestern in ye bathing room
   and the privy Kitchen

Pipes though full at the beginning   To get water
cannot be full in the end   swifte
              in aequall quantity
              withoute
              losse or dammage
              to the milles
    that drawe likewise on this river

Let there be more copy in a line of inclination, but add also
a syphon (weyght to be experimented)

Orbiguitie

I see a man in the Moone,
   Fie man, fie:
I see a man in the Moone,
   Who's the foole now?
I see a man in the Moone,
Clowting of Saint Peters shone,
   Thou hast well drunken man,
   Who's the foole now?

Much ado about *noh*t'n (*nut*'n) acted out
as shapes on a divers shore:

He fires paper bullets of the brain
as tobacco lifted to ayre

She sees abroad what's here at home
(better is a lover stufft)

      O giddie figure
      that's of little place
      and great

      a signe we skrebble
      like pipes of the voyce
      in a hexachord

It tells, this graine, faced in a blank
all about the white blew
round square sky

      how comes a thinge
      without start or ende

self-jarring and compackt

Jest Site

If you goe to Braynford a punke will have you to bed,
you shall pay as liberall as Caesar for Sacke & Sugar.
Yet you may mete who you will without after-buzze,
sit at Tables into night gaining muche from nought.

When the weather is rawish and cold a paire of Oares
will make foule speech as *Caron* hath taught them
but take you under tilt by swish or sway to anie reach
or miry bank while Westerne smelts like soules nibble.

Perchance the Meddowes of *Sion* will bid you practise
upon a Lute, which you must not breake in peces.
For this, with a sweete voyce or two over the rundle,
pluckes off baudie-traffike and puts all follie behinde.

Bide and Find

Experiments in a cleare & calme day from the leades.
of high. 43 ¼ foote. or 43 $\frac{25}{100}$ f.

In the fall:
lead & ~~cole~~ cherecoal. 6 & 9 foote a sunder. ⎞
lead & ~~wax~~ red wax. ½ & 1 foote.   ⎬ above 20 trialles
lead & Iron. scarce sensible difference.   ⎠
lead & half empty tobacco box of firre.—9 foote.

~~18~~ 24. cole = 1. leade.
8.   wax = 1. leade.
3.   iron = 1. leade.
lead & water aboute a foote asunder for that high
tried about 20 times though difficultly.
remember to try agayne.

   The proportion of ayer to lead. got by red wax.
8 of red wax is æquall to 1 of leade.
In the same time that lead falleth 43 $\frac{25}{100}$ feet *(f)*
Wax falleth abot ½ foote lesse, that is
   42 $\frac{75}{100}$ feet *(g)*

Let *(b)* be the weght or gradus &c . . .   so by æquation

         fall against fall   *

                                  *   in a *medium*
                                *

               will tell   its weght (relative)

                        Δ

         Glasse vessel luted & sealed.
         Heat by stages
         As hy as the line a bout the place
         where the glass beginneth to narrow
         there was sweating drops at the imposition,
         but all clear above.

I sate by

At 6^h: some brode scales of dew.
At 7^h: a fine misty dew of silver color
 up to the line b.
At 8^h: the hyest parte turning into drops.

$11\frac{1}{2}^h$: One N. 2 not far asonder. NE a big one.
S a letle One. SW. 2 greate ones.

12^h: one of the great drops fell which was SW
 & the other remayning, but seeming
 as he wold fall.

The drops from c to b ly upon the top
of the white and silver dew.

Ignis extingted.

   Terra.
   Glasse. Q.
  Coles. 7^h. 6ʹ. mane
  Nipped hor. $7\frac{1}{2}$
Imposition in terram. hor. 11^h. 30ʹ. AM.

Thyro-practike

The properties of the four elementes.
Mr Allens Book.
Varro.
My notes of ordinance.
Proclus de moto.

what would be the degree of motion
when a bodie throwne out
falls?

    poynt, pases
    within a trapeze or quadrangle

    shot diverse, theyr range
    in respecte of:

    wayte, heate of the peece
    windes ligne, thickenesse of ayre

The temper & quantity supposed to be one
and all other considerations alike,
what lawes applye?

Experimente: grossely, till better

Brayne Track

Worth the journey from Duresme house,
three hours upstream by a curling line
or 9 miles as the crowe (says
my instrument on the leades
12 foote long).

Syon reach, great quadrangular case
heaved from daughters' ruin.

A lone hernshaw, neck and legs stretched
flaps a powder wing in the shallows.
Horned cattle, a milk constellation
on Tide Meadow, mooze
before angle-turrets and gallery glass.

Waterstair. Ghost of Lady Jane.
Oars that dashed the creek
at rest. Winding path
to a neat walk with mulberries.

Think a whole 'arbal, knotly
layd to perfume the aire
in freaked order

    silverie wormewode
    branke-ursin
    whyte nesewurt
    dyshmustard
    panicke
    bellragges
    hore calamynt
    wood spurge
    chokefitche
    horse tyme
    cystbush
    purple goosegrass

▷

Sovereine and strang these Doctor Turner
found by the Temmes side
or planted, for physick
(a good tryal whereof in Latin
princess Elizabeth ventured
in now the Cherye garden or orchard
half an age back)

and he the healer under Somerset's cloak,
every day more vexed with the stone,
a man hot headed to know.

Smelts they swimme up to Thistelworth—
stronde of this side . . . Note from a stroll
away from swete-lipped town folk
for a booke of fishes, stones, metalles.

Anno '97: the rose quartered in a face
begins to fade. But a man arriving
treads white light—sand, gravel, steps, hall.

> Dye cubike with eye-shafts to the court
> that filled a cloister. Some wait till the earl
> will broach his plan. Then few words:
> a wave, a tag, a pewter goblet.

To Mr Heryott pension 80^{li}
as graft to stock
all subjects appliable.

Lodging & laboratory,
a small house apart, at the tip
of the wall from her la: shipp's towre.
Landskip to burn away dross
as in the scale one mean
turns *gentle*man. Owly-eyed, black-suited
magister of Braynford, magus
furnished wth

great leather-cov^d globes,
chests of bookes of all sorts,
furnaces in the lybrarie closetts,
longe table piled with papers.

Under the white crescent or half-moon
the *Percy* sign
neither servant nor officer

a skull can open.

Hands unclasp to liquid gauge
the trail of stuff, its cast and rate
by pulses and paternosters.

Will you familiar rise
from the chimney-place,
chase some reason for a little event
with upright parabola, numbers split by a bar.

The heron climbs, slow and heavy,
swings along and swoops. A frog, a snake?
no, a silver fish.

Crosscut

To the Water-gate stayres at Mortlak,
neere and of light cost.

Mr Dee has seen my Lanterne,
wherein a burning candle may be carried
in stormie or windie weather.

He telles me Mr Saunders of Ewell
sent home his great sea cumpas
but without a needle. It cam in the night
by water.

Navigation & angels: one opticke
kept from spoilation.

He holds course, back of the court
bereaved of bokes or the great nomber.
In an *appendix practical* some Stilles going
by a payle of Eggeshells.
Ruine of that olde project, limits unseene.

He has now the next mansion howse
with the plat and the hovel on the other.
Has hope againe of her Majesty's favour,
as help to St Crosses.

Mistress Dee angry, in respect of her maydes
(the kitchen smalle). He has had
a fit of the stone in his left kydney.
Drinks a draught of white wyne and salet oyle,
and after that, crabs' eys in powder
with the bone in the carp's head.

To his late library-roome,
proximal ghost of that shalbe called agayne.
Walks the passage with fuzzed edges:
upright, handes behind him,
beard picked, a white arrow.

He pulls from his cedar-wood chest
the sheet with signes. All not dumb
we agree.

I do not see them immortall
yet those rates of waights, forces, times
may be expressed by lines.

We try continually, marking the performance
of thinges. Pipes and spowts . . . What difference
between an angel and a separated soule?

Outlandish & homish,
the letters in the squares
do dance. *Doctor* D your diall and glyphs
deliver the rasher solution
sometimes Better.

When we argue it is well:
the gall (as plied) goes thick and thin.

These wordes are written
    with *China* inke.
But these are written with *London* inke.

290

Cause, Beginning and One

In principio fecit Deus caelum et terram
Gen. lib 1

All questions regarding the spirit
must be resolved: what they can knowe,
what is possible and impossible to knowe.

> *I am the Beginning* (Jesus)   John 8.25
> *He* (the devil) *a murderer from the beginning*   John 8.44

What if God is not the Creator but a creature?
Can he be absolute emperor of the Spirites?
or are there *many* rulers?

Socrates sayd he knewe nothinge
and Aristatus sayd he knew not as much as that
and pyrho and his followers make there knowledge
certayne to dout assuredly.

What *light* is let in time? And stuffe from nothing
that is smalle partes eternal.

> To venture at discourse
> in the boosome of the citie,
> in her out skirtes or farre-off waies,
> is to set all on hazard: friends that smile
> may, through envie, turne the cat in the pan.

Opinion comes a gladsome guest to get thinges
from nought—one word bolstered frames a tale.

How is this eargot at first forme? A mott might hang
that fathomes his decree by surquedry.

So, guard the doore of thy mouth
from they that lie close.

Godsip

Touchyng Sr W. Rawley's Schoole of Atheisme
where in both the olde and the new Testamente
are jested at, and schollers taught
amonge other thinges to spell God backwarde.

Some hath harde them saye:

That the Indians & many Authors of antiquity
have assuredly writen of above 16,000 yeares agone
wher at Moyses Adam is said proved to have lived
within 6 thowsand yeares.

That Moyses was but a Jugler, & that one Heriots
being Sr W. Raleighs man can do more than he.

That the first beginning of Religion was only
to keep men in awe, that there is no Hel or misery
but opinion.

That Jhesus christe was a bastarde, Saint Mary
a whore & the Aungell Gabriell a bawde
to the holy ghoste. Christ was Justly persecuted
for his owne foolishnes.

That the apostles were fellows
neither of wit nor worthe, that Paule
was a timorous fellow in bidding men
be subject to magistrates against conscience.

That if there be any god or any good Religion
it is in the papists because the service of god
is performed with more ceremonies,
as Elevation of the mass, organs, singing men,
shaven crownes, &c.

That if Christ would have instituted the sacrament
with more ceremoniall Reverence it would have
bin had in more admiration, that it would have bin
better being administered in a Tobacco pipe.

▷

That we can not lerne what god is
or what is this ens entium. For one principle
in mathematickes—as *the whole is lesse
than its partes*—may be turned, to showe
in the table in the window in a man
the whole is bigger than the partes of it.

That in seeking Truthe men should not be afeard
of bug beares and hobgoblins.

That the Conjuror that is M[aster] thereof
had as good right to coine as the Queen,
that he had learned from one Poole
the mixture of mettals, and ment to coin
ffrench crownes pistolets & English shillings.

———————

*Can saye nothinge of my owne knowledge
but speake from generall reporte.*

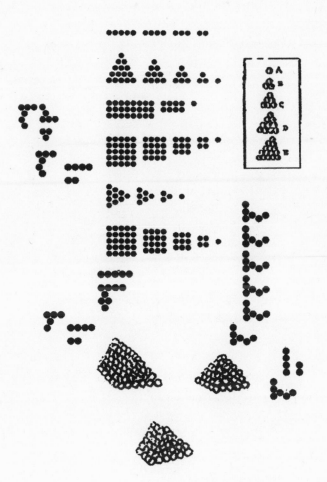

Sundri Poyntes

What way best to pile cannon bullets
(as on deck, to Virginia)

the pyramid

O
ball to
ball laide
hony-combe
like, tessella fytt
on speciall three or
four sided ground plat

Lattice-lock yron quick to be seized
(twice said once)

You must know:
how many in every ranke
and how many rankes

then by rule the nomber of bulletes
there conteyned

Here I lay oute a table (divers
suited), a slide charde
to read acrosse

toppe against key diagonall, *so:*

the nomber downe the side (of four)
being 7, the total is 140

. . . .

Farther: there must be a cause
why snowe has the shape
of a six-cornered starlet

```
          flake
       fall   tuft
       skeleton
       adorn
```

small enough to be naught (*nix*)
stirs some reason (unseen)

why a grayne and his neighbours
          in bodye-packe
          are so disposed

this site   of others
          the mirrour

as baubles   float   on mercury

now   in present case   the print
familiar   of dayes remote
I thinke   I see

it is   not settled   the litle solides
from nothing   cluster and arace

    Can you believe   what
you scan   flickers   a meanes
for   dare defy(ne) such

        the solution of all

Circle Stuffe

For spirit of wyn.   d. Turn$^{r.}$
Und$^{r.}$ A. a fyr to rayz flem and spirit:
Und$^{r.}$ B. a gent. fyr to rese the flem.
tip up [t]he spirt [t]hat it may pas into C

lewt.

Furst tak a fat clay, and al to bet it
with convenyent instriwments
til it bi so wel wrowt as any poters muwld
and in wurking of it cler it ov al stonz,
hwen yow hav it so, then fil it az ful of flokz
as may bi til it bi of a [g]od consistans,
then put in so mucl [s]and or brik
as wil mak it not cleving to yor hand./
[t]he comon menstruwim iz watr
[t]he nekst iz al[e] drenk
[t]he best iz solt watr

doct^{r} Turnr
septembr. 1590.

Floating Canto

The giddy M oone says
we go here U nperfite as
halfe-ripe T urneppes
that cannot A dvance mid
grounde like B ogges on top
of mountains I f anie track be
founde in blue L it glinnes then
wolves, thieves I nsare & frett us
for nothing long S tands in one stay

Still within grete C hange a sorte of
ever rules (one O ke disbowel'd
uglie wormes N ousle and all
raines waste ● yet bravelye
yong plants S pring from
her rinde T o restocke
natures A ccompt
for sunne N ourisheth
this wilde S pun stage

Quietz Rampart

Stone, hammered from sky-toppe
holds up quike, with grey lichen
drape.

A little Troy with oozy ribs
you cannot fathome.

My rumbelo kindred: blustrous ghospell
of a chanted hour, one
gosse-hawke at the window.

Stick to your tacklings,
the words throb far in passage.

Apart from any fyrebroil
I work at the meanes to endure,
with a box of grene gynger
for ringdance and badge pipes.

Turffe smoaks by a nouke.
Usqubagh keeps the throte from ratling.

Molana

Am I here a god or devill
at the bulbous elbow
on Blackwater

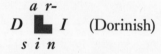 (Dorinish)

You can patch and refit
a shipwracke cloyster,
keep a fyre all winter
beneath Oake beams
and write

ashlar grooves
on rose-red,
a velvett cushion
by the wall
where crying sinnes
were heard

with now a pastyme
of tales
after fishe-stew
from the weir

There waits a medley of trees
for measure,
then barren grounde

You might face a stone
dropt from a battlement,
you might miss a plate of meate
when you're called to butt & bound

All despite, 'I' quoiles into 'They'
echoes *Awemore*—apparent
through lots disjoyned

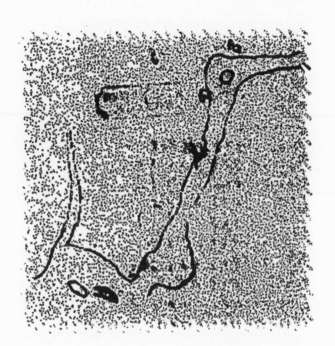

Alterage

It is demanded where their cows are,
it is demanded when the wood kerne meet,
it is demanded how the land is named.

Assume one ballibetagh is 950 acres *(acrabh)*
or, say, a thousand.
That you may parcel out and fix.

> No, a *baile baittaig* is however much land
> will support 300 cows
> or yield so many (agreed) ploughing days

> Or it's a place held to do service.

What fruits & commodities?

> All is swordland now, every screed
> in a milk-rich plain.

There is *termon* land, which is to saye
that free of overlordship
because a *corbe* or prior has it
or else some *herinach* or clerk has it
preserving the soul's health
of this church's founder.

Other lands are chargeable, and bear
sorren or *soirthean* (quarterage),
cuddy (a night's portion),
cosherie (visitation),
cess (spoilinge)—
performed in kinde or waived for a fee.

Trim for better usage.

> Who will buy a poem
> if dealings fall
> to a boorish clod?

They have a whyning tune in their speech
as if they did still smart or suffer some oppression.

Strange words we must knowe, yet not so
we drink of Circe's cup and become like them.

> *In eol duit bérla do lavairt*
> Cann you speake Inglishe?

> *abair ladden*
> speake Latten?

> *Gath haad o showh go port laarg*
> How farre is it to Waterford?

> *Toor yeske*
> Gyve me some fyshe!

> *Hewen, dow, tre, kaar*
> One, two, three, foure.

Deliver it *shogh* (here).

They call her Highness *Banryne done*
(brown-haired or naughty Queene).

They are great swillers of Spanish sacke,
which they call the king of Spaynes Daughter
(*iníon Rí na Spáinne*).

They cry out that their *garrans* and *caples*
are taken—*bohbowe, lullalowe.*

We may give them words, to enjoy
their estate:

> *contributions*   taxes
> *gardes*   garrisons
> *houses*   prisons

dream they should not turne
like a Game at Irish.

Field Book

Wood-howsed or open, a chayne-man
stamps each plat, drags his iron
to get the stuffe in sum.

First I would know this great dot
in a rolling flood, its angles
and mass, as more than a ghesse—
the fertile waste that eyes might daze.

How? at edge of craft
with absent gear.

25 spannes is a pole in length.
625 square spannes is a pole square.
16 pole is a square of the whole chaine
or 1 tenth of an acre
or: a daye worke.

We put the pieces into one
by *prosthaphaeresin* (sines added
to finde a product).

So walk the mind, sufficiently exacte.

Plantation

Plot the shape of the lande and dwellings
and you have halfe in your hand
what's contained and what will come.

First drawe the largest possible rectangle,
then a series of triangles within
and so resolve.

This part lyeth faire upon the Ocean:
the rivers go east betweene ridges
then drop to the maine-sea, as if magnetick.

Some would be baulked
by quagmires and stonie hills
with showers, mist or sunne-shafts.
Yet you will finde the cooly shade
of green alders and spatious places
with streames full of fish.

There is much good timber, and Oke
of that streightnesse that is good to reave.
You may cutt barrel & hogshead bords
for our cuntrie, and so enterteyne men in worke.

The people are beyond measure proud
and do hate bondage, they have tough bodies
and love musicke. Though dispersed
and in a maner mounstrous
they will creep back.

You may keep a better house here
for L. li. a yeere, than in England for CC. li.

Linked Saws

Whosoever commands the Sea,
commands the Trade.
Whosoever commands the Trade of the world,
commands its Riches
and so the world it selfe.

Spayne seeks not Irlande for Irlande
but, having raysed up troops of beggars
in our backs, shall inforce us
to cast our eyes over our shoulders
while those before us
strike us on the braynes.

There must be watchinge and wardinge:
here is that deep harborough
where your shipps may lie fytt for service.
If commanded by ordnance
from walles and towres at either side,
no enemie shal gain holde.

For the sute of Lesmore the Queen
will dismis cavelations.
If my builders want, supply them.

Sir Walt: Ralegh

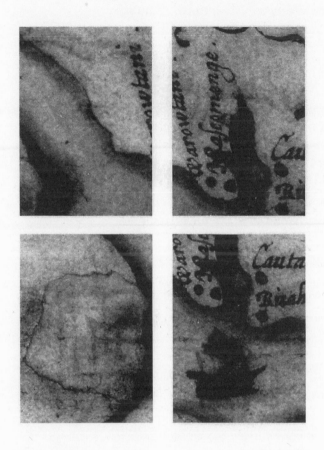

In Nomine

Ark Rawlye   Deptford, June 1587
                from Mr Chapman his yard—
by art with workemanlye care
sholde carry suche grace and countenaunce
as to terrorize the enemie.

Arke-royall   To her Majestie, January 1588
                in liewe of 5,000*li*, deabt—
for that morrice-daunce upon our waves
(this ile opprest) I thinke her
the odd shipp in the worlde for all conditiones:
no other shall make me goe out.

Anne Royal   Woolwich Dock, 29 September, 1608
                in the charge of Phineas Pett
her name re-caste by Sir Oliver Cromwell
dispight of the Kings neglect.

An hundreth foote by the keele
and thirtye seven foote broad
now sum deale overpestred & cloggd:

    demy Cannon   4
    Cannon perrier   4
    Culverin   12
    demy Culverin   16
    Saker   6
    port Peece   4
    Fowler   4

Adamant to clappe a reckninge
that fludds agayne, smoak Morblew
through manghangled trobles.

One ghost a way from the firme slydes
sulphure suted at the close
with a shrugge of octoretye:

Bilged on her ancor, the Medway, 1636.

Searching Fume

There is an herbe which is sowed a part by it selfe
in moyst and shadow places
& is called *vppówec*:
the leaves thereof being dried
& brought into powder
they use to take the fume or smoke thereof
by sucking it thorough pipes made of claie
into their stomacke and heade
from whence it purgeth superfluous fleame
& other grosse humors, openeth
all the pores & passages of the body,
which use preserveth the body from obstructions.
Whereby they know not many greevous diseases
wherewithall wee in England are afflicted.

Sometimes they make hallowed fires
& cast some of the pouder therein
for a sacrifice: being in a storme uppon the waters
to pacifie their gods they cast some up
into the aire & into the water:
so a weare for fish being newly set up
they cast some therein & into the aire:
also after an escape from danger
they cast some into the aire likewise:
but all done with strange gestures,
stamping, sometime dauncing,
clapping of hands, holding up of hands
& staring up into the heavens
uttering and chattering strange words & noises.

One will fall doune uppon the ground
as a dedde manne
and when the hearbe has doen his woorke
he does revive & awake
and in any maner of businesse
will interprete as he is consailed.

▷

We were used to suck it after their maner
as also since our returne & have found
manie rare & wonderfull experiments
of the virtues thereof, of which
the relation woulde require a volume by it selfe:
the use of it by so manie of late,
men & women of great calling as else
and some learned Phisitions also,
is sufficient witness.

Devills Alphabet

How to recorde these mouthed wordes
on paper? That others may knowe
what sense runnes, not hiding I venture
the partes of a name: *TH/HT, o <—> a, mr*
the letters curlde and crossed, wrastling gleames,
or edged with a Trident, no fowle conceite
to marke its tonge-waye

as here on the river in noting discarde
Manteo and *Wanchese*, oure two Indians
like white Moors change skinnes
for brown taffeta.

Shewed up and downe for wonder
they have not high-spriggd fethers,
stravagant, estrangefull, but woodborne
draw spots from shadowes.

Thamse side a bended moon offers one hall
with marble pillars, gaynward the gravell & drifte.

Should these stares trip you to speake
like Sea Crabs, what Mockado is not
in men who remove from straiter places?
Lord above Bull, Beare and Horse: chuse you
the head or butt, soe the lip will jig
Spin, span, muskidan. If I becomes it,
some other that's tagged, who is then
the gem-tell man?

Just such brabling businesse doth slide
a Squirt-Rime, with sayles of scarlet & gold
caryed from Blake Wale to Greenwych.

Tar-mowse heere-eie-ought
standes by grace of Dasamonguepeuk
as muche a layd spektacle.

* * * * *

[An universall Alphabet conteyninge
six & thirty letters, whereby may be
expressed the lively image of mans voyce
in what language soever; first devised
upon occasion to seeke for fit letters
to expresse the Virginia speche. 1585]

A table of certayne wordes which do
expresse their power; which power
they are to hold generally in all places
where they are written.

⟨⟩ as (a) in   all, tall, fall, call.
⟨⟩ as (o) in   ore, for, core.
⟨⟩ as (a) in   arruw, man, pan.
⟨⟩ as (u) in   us, upon, but, cut.
⟨⟩ as (a) in   ape, ale, any, are.
⟨⟩ as (e) in   erbe, end, the.
⟨⟩ as (i) in   ise, ire, pipe.
⟨⟩ as (e) in   he, she.
    or (ee) in   thee, eele.
⟨⟩ ⎱ in barbarouse words only, & not to be
⟨⟩ ⎰ expressed but viva voce.
⟨⟩ as (o) in   so, no, otes.
⟨⟩ as (o) in   do, to, shoe.

⟨⟩ as (y) in   yea, yes, day.
⟨⟩ as (w) in   way, was, now, sow.
⟨⟩ as (r)   roofe.
⟨⟩ as (l) in   lake.
⟨⟩ as (z) in   zone, zachery.
⟨⟩ as the french (j) in   je, jeter.
    or as (g) in   hodge, judge.
⟨⟩ as (s) in   sault, samon.
⟨⟩ as (sh) in   she, shoe.

⟨⟩ as (m) in   man.
⟨⟩ as (n) in   not.
⟨⟩ as (ng) in   king, thing, fling, or (n) in knave.
⟨⟩ as (v) in   vine, geve.
⟨⟩ as (th) in   the, thine, these.

⟨⟩ as (gh) in some barbarouse wordes.

⟨⟩ as (f) in fling, feare, of.

⟨⟩ as (th) in thing, thorne.

⟨⟩ as (ch) in some barbarouse words or as
      the Greeke χ.

⟨⟩ as (h) in hat, he, oh.

⟨⟩ as (b) in borde, but.

⟨⟩ as (d) in do, drudge, good.

⟨⟩ as (g) in good, god, gebe, hog.

⟨⟩ as (p) in pan, &c.

⟨⟩ as (t) in tooth, to, ten, hat.

⟨⟩ as (c) in corne or as (k) in keep &c.

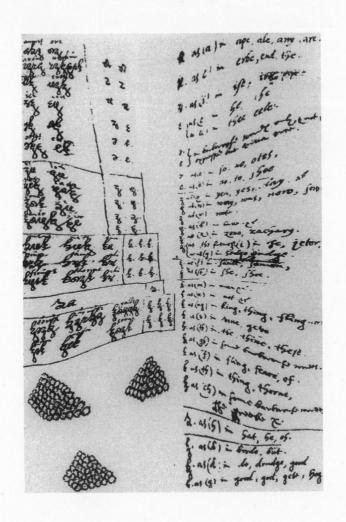

Eare Witnesse

Wechêkum	The Sea.
Mishoonémese	A little Canow.
Kitênuck	A Ship.
Wuskon-tógwhan	It will goe adrift.
Cuttánnummous	I will help you.
Pakétenish	Let goe or let flie.
Nikkoshkowwaûmen	We shall be drown'd.
Maumaneeteántass	Be of good courage.
Kínnequass	Steere.
Awêpesha	It caulmes.
Tamóccon	Floud.
Awánick Paûdhuck	Who comes there?
Asképunish	Make fast the Boat.
Caupaushess	Goe ashoare.
Neene Cuthomwock	Now they goe off.
Npenowauntawâumen	I cannot speake your language.
Cuppítous	I understand you.
Ahânu	Hee laughes.
Wunnáumwash	Speake the truth.
Takekummûo	Is there a Spring?
Yo áinshick méyi	There the way lies.
Teâno wouck nippéeam	I will be here by and by againe.
Waútacone-nûaog	Englishman, men. That is coat-men.
Cháuquaquock	English-men, properly sword-men.
Neesquttónckqussu	A babler, or prater.
Nummautanùme	I have spoken enough.
Matta mihtuckqunnuno	Have you no trees?
Wesássu	Afraid,
Cowésass	Are you afraid?
Tawhitch wesásean	Why feare you?
Manowêsass	I feare none.
Kukkushickquock	They feare you.
Nosemitteúnckquock	They fly from mee.
Onamatta cowaûta	Let us pursue.
Nuckquasha	I feare him.

▷

Wussémo-wock	He flies, they flie.
Npauchíppowem	I flie for succour.
Keesaúname	Save me.
Npúmmuck	I am shot.
Chenawaú	Churlish.
Waumaûsu	Loving.
Tawhitch chenawaûsean	Why are you churlish?
Aumánsk	A Fort.

A little Key may open a Box, where lies a bunch of Keyes.

I drew the materialls in a rude lumpe at Sea, as
a private helpe to my owne memory, that I might
not lightly lose what I had so dearely got.

I laboured to suite my endeavours to my pretences:
and (out of desire to attaine their Language) ran
through varieties of Intercourses with them Day and
Night, Summer and Winter, by Land and Sea.

They say that they have sprung and growne up in that
very place, like the very trees of the wildernesse.

By occasion of their frequent lying in the Fields
and Woods, they much observe the Starres, and
they have the same words for their rising, courses
and setting, as for the Sunne or Moone.

The Wildest sons of Men heare the preaching
of the Heavens, the Sun, Moone, and Starres,
though they deny not an other God.

At our last parting, I closed with one concerning his Soule.
He said: 'me so big naughty Heart, me heart all one stone.'

Unpaynted Table

What is that? (pointing)
the place (over your shoulders)
how say you this?

Wingandacon
=
You weare gay clothes
(or)
balsom-firre,
yeeldes a sweete-smel

So the name is set downe

Wingandacoia
Wigandecua

Virginia

* * *

Stand close to the glasse
and thinges are as they are.

Step back and they growe big.

Set the glasse farther from you
then the burninge beam
and trees, hilles, shippes on the water
hange upside down.

They think it *god-worke.*

Other

They (voyde of all covetousness)
lyve cherfullye, at their harts ease
with Deere skins rounde their middles,
all els naked.

Their townes are small
and neere the sea coast but fewe
and compassed abowt with smale poles
stock thick together.

What makes this plentie
I could rehearse:—

Mangúmmenenauk, the acorne of their oak,
which boiled may be eaten in stead of bread.

Winauk (or Sassafras), a wood of swete smel
that they use to cure greevous deseases.

Seékanauk, a kinde of crustie shel fishe,
Tortoyses (ougly but good meate).

Oyle (of Walnuttes and of Beares, commonly fatte),
Pearle (of which one man made a fayre chaine).

Wine (the lande being so full of grapes
as the very beating & surge of the Sea
overflowes them).

Let those briefes suffice.

Points Performed

There runneth from the West a most notable River
with many creeks and turnings, for thirtie miles
as broad as the Thames betwixt Greenwich
and the Ile of dogges.

We did ask what traffike there is
and what store may be found.

The mineral they say is *Wassador* (copper)
but they call by that name every mettall
whatsoever. They take it out of the river
that falls swift from hie rocks and hyls,
letting into a bowle as much oare
as can be held, which presently they cast
into a fire.

It is twentie dayes journey, the last parte by land.
We started forth but after five dayes voyage
there came from the shoare a song
that Manteo knewe as signe of battell
and there lighted a vollie of arrowes among us.

Having passed deep into that Countrey
we were nowe come to our dogs porredge,
two mastives with sassafras leaves.
We determined to be going backe againe
and so rowed downe the currant to the mouth,
from where after great winde & billow
we arrived at our home Roanoake.

Nothing els but the discovery of a good mine
or a passage to the Southsea or someway to it
can bring this country to be inhabited
by our nation. With such discovery it will be
the most sweete and healthfullest climate
and the most fertile soyle, being manured
in the world.

Air Sweep

A rare & strange accident moved the countrey
that either knew or hearde of us
to wonderfull admiration:

There was no towne where wee
had any subtile devise practised against us
but that within a few dayes after our departure
people began to die, many in short space,
the disease so strange that they neither knew
what it was, nor how to cure it.

Those that were immediatly to come after us
they imagined to be in the aire
yet invisible & without bodies
& that they by our intreaty did shoot
the people with invisible bullets.

Their phisitions
to excuse not curing the disease
would make people beleeve
that the strings of blood they sucked out
were those wherewithall the bullets
were tied and cast.

Exchange Notes

We sought to allure them by gyftes,
then with our drummes and trumpetts
but they, supposing this a signe of battayle,
left their oars and put arrows to their bowes.
Yet drawing nearer the shippe they saw us
looke cheerfully on them. They called awhile
their spirites, then heard againe
our whoall noyse, with flutes and shaulmes,
and were dumme & amazed
at that sweete harmony.

From their canowe they climbed aboard,
wonderynge at all, tackelinges & such.
Our captain made offer of a bell in his hande
and they were greatly delighted
with this brighte thing that giveth a sounde.
A youth in our company played upon a gitterne
and sang *O man where is thy hart*
and they gave in turne a Tobacco-pipe
and a Snakes skinne.

They danced in a ring, with Savage gestures,
singing *Io, Ia, Io, Ia, Ia, Io*: him that brake the ring
the reste would knock and cry out upon.
We founde they have many barbarous tunes,
pretty to them as a Country-round
plaied by our pipe and tabor.

By this musicke we had friendly imbracings:
they strooke the breasts of our companie
and theyr owne. For goode will we gave them
a shirte, two table napkins and aquavitae.
And one of them blowing in the bottle, yt made
a sound, at which they fell into a laughture.

Entryes and Portes

Which gap to chuse
in this endlesse bank of bony sand?

Grope warily for a meanes
to go in
to sume delycate and swete provynce.

First looms *Wococon*,
port of saynt maris
the Spanish saye

there you lye beatynge upon ye shoale
with extreme hasarde of beying casteawaye.

Better is *Porte FerdiNando*,
found by our Pylotte maggiore
which hathe a barre also
but very shorte,
being within iii, iiij, and v fathom water
so you may ride it.

Last, to the north
is Trynytye harboroughe
that is only of viij foote
upon the barre at hyghe water.

Anie charte undoes a line strod
with brine-caked eies,
you get there and the figure slips
in another surge.

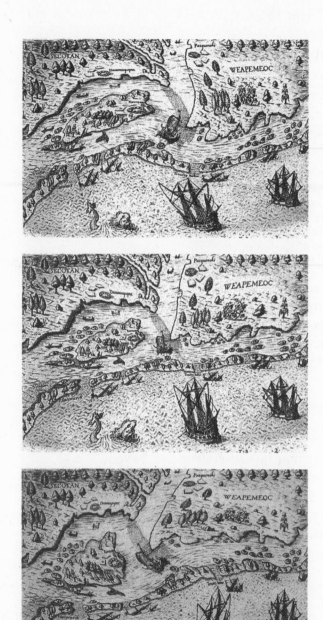

A First Seate

To safelye arrive & plante one self
uppon an Ilande in the mouth
of some notable river, or upon the poynt of the lande
entring into the river, if no such Iland be—
this were to great ende.

Then can you shift into lande that is spatious
(I would not saye voyd).
See how in your traffique with the people
they are tractable, as by trifles
they will give or disclose
that worth our care.

Every soyle of the world by arte may be made
to yeelde things to feede and to cloth.
Bring in your returne a perfect note of the soyle
and we shall devise if neede require
to cary thither such other plants
as yeelde reliefe.

Drawe to life what is strange
so we may fitly marvell or fear, beyond
the smoake of our owne chimneyes.

Above all, do not advertize the killing
of any of your men, that the countrie people
may know it.

———

Notes for Master Rauleys viage:
That no Indian be forced to labor unwillingly
That no Souldier do violat any woman
non shall stryke or mysuse any Indian
non shall Enter any Indians howse without his leave

Register

sharres in warre

8. Captayne   Leiuttennant 6.
7. Master   Auncient
6. mastermates, 2   Sarjeant
4. Quarter masters, 4. to looke to the   Corporall   3.
      grande table & romage in holde   Soldiers   1.
      to looke to the watches, & for
      to call the men to the helme   Drummers
                                         Trumpeters

4. Boteswayne
3. Boteswaynes mate
5. Midshipmen   All starbord men
2. Mariners   Surgeon   on the masters side
1. Yonkers   & larbord men
$\frac{1}{2}$ Boyes   on the mates side
2. or $4\frac{1}{2}$ Swabbar   or on bothe mates sides
1. Swabbers mate
5, or 4 Master Gunner
4 or 3 His mate
2.2$\frac{1}{2}$ Quarter Gunners   A watch is:
2. Gunners   8 glasses $= \frac{8}{2}$ houres
                                          $= 4$ houres
5.4 Purser   The watch from 4 to 8 at night
3. Steward   is devided into two partes:
2. Cooper   the later parte from 6 to 8
4.3 Cook & his mate   they call the *looke out*.

Cape Marchant, in steed of the captayne in Marchentes
             Marchantes or Factors
1. Shifters (of vituayle,)

These two parts are as two watches,
that the same men may not have the first watch.
The first watch beginnes at 8 at night;
then they set the watch.
     1. watch
     2. watch
     Day watch, or morning watch.

A competent number, all sortes of commodities fitting—
the half to watch & worke
whilest the others sleepe, and take rest

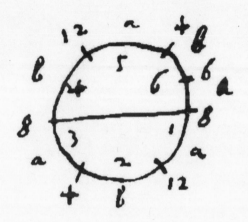

Addes

First lay the Keele, a great tree or more.
Skarf into it the Stemme, let in the Starne post
somewhat sloping: from it doth rise
2 fashion peeces, a paire of great hornes.
Bind the beames with good knees,
upright or oblike. Then lay all the Flore timbers,
trenneld, and cut your Limberholes above the keele.

In that frame: the first futtock &c
(straddle or struddle by some of the contry)
draws a sweep to the soothmarke.

The seconde bendes flore timber must stand
so farre off that the futtocke may come betweene
with some advantage.

When too much is cut away in beveling
they put in a shame wedge.

In making of the mould from the flat floor
is specially to be considered the hanging off
of the side, for which they have no certayne rule
but judgement of the ey,
these thinges being considered:
the holding of goodes, the sayling, & bearing.

If a shippe be not sheathed
it may be eaten. What starts a small Spanish Needle
growes greater then a mans finger.

Goat hayre, pitch, tarre or tallow
with some simple pouder of glasse
below the waterline
discomfits the worme
(they pay on the stuffe with mappes).

Over which may be nayled thin bourds,
Elme being better then Oake

▷

for it ryveth not and yeeldeth better
to the Shippes side.

All is out to the better end
they say (bitter is a stopper).

To bring her upon the careen is to lay her
upon one side on the water
that the garbell strake (shaver next the keele)
may be calked.

No pitcht place without calking
can suffer the force & peaze of the water,
in neglect whereof, *mem.* a trivuell–hole
in the post left open.

A luffe ~~in the winde~~: to stay her in the wind
                                to hinder her way.

The rut (roaring) of the sea.
Disimboage, a gulph, the froth of the sea.
An eddy wind, a flake of wind, a Herycano.

Shee lyes downe like a crab
            (when shee will not bear sayle)
Shee is a crabsided thing.

Shee is very thyte. not leaky
        as thyte as a fish
Shee is stanch (of the stinking water of the
                    pumpe I thinke)
wee drinke more then we pomp.

Fooke sayle
(a plugge. a stopple.)   I skite well but plump not.

Shee is limber sicke: the limbers are stopped
& then the keel rope is to clere it.

These are the chief propertyes of a ship in the sea.
To go well, to stear well & beare a good sayle.

Plotte the figures by which *all* (?) is subject
that proportion with arte agrees: a scale
not a brabble of cyphers cast up & down
a thousande thousande fold. Manie may peruse
few that wil us knowe.

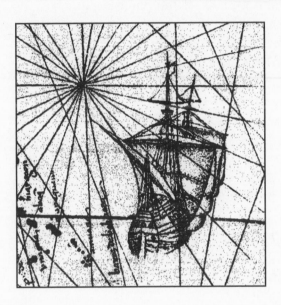

Arcticon

To make Terra nova: a little turret
over the Thames, with entrance on to the leades

Had not my chamber these and a spoute
in the corner, the rayne that falleth
would reach $268\frac{3}{4}$ foote square

My cube of brasse whose internall side 3 inches
conteyneth of rayne water
just full by eye as it is even by the sides
& playned by a ruler ounces of
troye $\quad 14 \pm \frac{1}{2} \pm \frac{1}{16}$

The leakes being stopped, it is full
with just $\quad$ troy $\quad 14 \pm \frac{1}{2}$

A beat of the pulse one second gives
$8\frac{1}{2}$ inches p. 24 hr

Calls the brain to fathom
how traverse on fish-track, stickle current
a vaster league
in growley squall & thicke fogge

Your rutter hath not the cutts
your almanack may not tally
nor compasse fall right

How to know your course to sayle
to any place assigned
& in sayling to keep to make true reckoning
to find where you are
& how farre from any place desired

Surplus of the Horizon (table in minutes)
to correct for the Hight of the ey
above the water in pases (one pase being 5 foot).
Elevation of the pole from meridian altitude of the Sonne.
A figure shewing when the guardes are in rule.

Allowances of the pole starre.
Regiment of the Sonne.
Amplitudes of the Sonne.

The astrolabe, his agitation & unquiet hanging.
The sea ringe's scale twice as large
but tossed again. Excentricity of the staffe.

By sea marriadge these will agree
as sonne & starre
and more nearly p.fect a maryners plot

Strand Reach

```
                A
            L       V
          A           I
        R               E
        G               W
        N               I
        S               N
        T               T
        H               O
        O               &
          G               O
          H               V
            T   THE       E
              THAMES       R


              T
          M   U   H
          A   R   O
        TIP DURHAM U
          H   E   S
          S   T   E
              C
              H
              A
              M
              B
              E
              R
```

Water Act

A well compacted person
with a bould and plausible tongue

    would write
    in a glas window

Fain would I climbe, yet feare to fall

    then get the reply

If thy heart faile thee, climbe not at all

    so a captaine
    will finde fabricke

a cloke by which to crosse over
a plashy place

withoute mirakell or fancye

    he who has
    the meanes

must by winde and tide
touch what promises best

Fore Pulse

Towne of oyster voices—*what do you lacke*,
cages for birdes, silver basons,
billyard balls, beards of all ages,
a carpet wrought of Paraquitos feathers.

Thinges to be wrapd in a title-leafe,
a pyke slit open to shew its fat guttes.

Such a thronge and presse as houses
scrape the sky and shippes stand
big as castles.

They that have got a glas in their heades
climb a tower to ring bells for houres,
for the sake of exercise. With like drummes
and firing of cannon.

Some streetes paved with limestone & flint,
others oozie, gouged by carts & horses,
a scummy chanel with Paracelsian bubbles.

At the Beargarden a rose is fixed, to be set on fire
by a rocket, soe that apples & peares
fall on the persons below.
Farther in that quarter are little roomes
where you maye get your bone smirched.

If these folk scoffe and laugh at a stranger,
your skilles will lette you precell them
and soare like a bridge over Thames his torrent.

Tamise Primer

Tunic open to spring, a man will get down
to the Bridge-foot, hear curses

churned, then sluggish, liquid in the vaines
and direction too

they say Bacon saw the starres
from this Pharos or Watch Tower
by the third arch

but—Body of god—at Graundpont
who can tell the osiers of the *Temmes*
all on a weave?

push back weeds, slide over shelves and shoales
(the Swift ditch is a better course)

there are piles will almost cleave
a barges bottome

at 5*d.* boats are towld as bells
by mill-damme, flash lokke, fish-weare,
that water ingrossed for private use

you might cut a loop—go jolted
in a wagon to Burcot, hand over wharfgelt
and strike out

through forced ilands and gurges
from Witnum to Maydenhed, a chain of esses
fed from plaschsy berall—a rillet laborinth—
with Chilton marl

row, steere, drive the prow
down elbow and arme,
spill without cable or wintch
to drop a level
as sun falls

flote under boughs at Mapledoreham
aside one rype, then swing wide
to low medowes, champain
before woodyd hilles

wildflower waves, primrose
and hare-bell, bakside of a garden
to the creek, lodging
by madrigal murmure
at the signe of the Crowne

Wyndsore: stone-skinned towers, deer
half-hydd beneath oak,
a game of swannes on a small aight
(diamond-figured gaze)

Stanes to Lallum guls, where vildly puzzled
you could turn broadside on,
next Chertseye's bridge askew, made
by left-handed men

drift with craft discharged, a crowd
at the double mouth before Otelands

Hampton, Kingston, Richemond
by farther curls, tyde-ruled—
the fludd courted to icy seas
and corridors that throb
a thousande thoughts & desires,
one grete mercate

wherryes, barges, skiffes intercrossing
the broad streame, grey-brown
into spottyd glintes burst,
a thickett of tackle and furniture

stretched catlings, peg heds
sound for silver: a stronge twang dang

▷

Sculler and scholar, once againe
put on a black velvet joope, leap ashore
at Milford Stairs or Puddle Wharfe
to the flintie street

crunch, cloppe, bang, buzze

Trolle on awaye:
Oysters, three pence a peck.
Will you buy any inke?
Soop, chimnay soop.
Touch and goe.

Subterrane Kalendar

Pan–cake Bell   of St Marie's
at 10 Clock   not the Great
for one has died
                all bitter words
dropt   as fresh Schollers
       pluck off gowne & band
to plead   on table-forme
nott fulminate   or tonitruate
but kisse   the shoe
to get   a cup of cawdel
or   if dull
    nothinge but salted beere
  with tucks to boot

so who'll wag out in towne
     a Brazen–Nose
  go buffeting

beef and bacons   oute of season
I want a pan   to parch my peason

no sconsing   as stones
     they hurle
   at dores

no tart satyr   of a magick pen
    we'll caste
    under the Postern gate

dillie dilli dawbes   one darke sollace

  All the maides in Soningewell
  you maye putt in an Eg-shelle

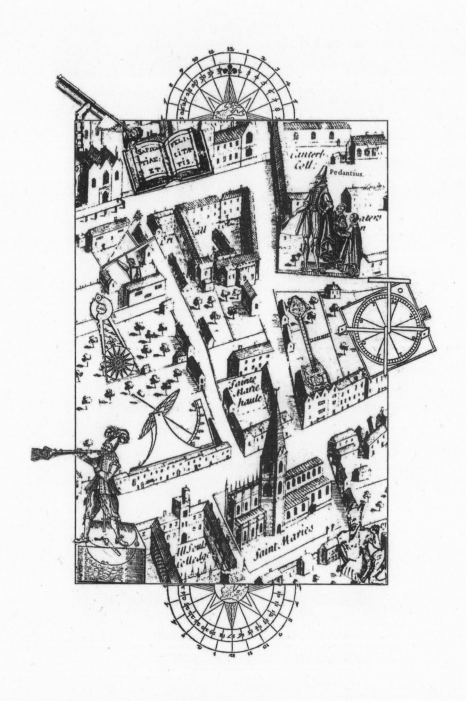

Told Over

A meanes to read the World, flatland
sprung, to beholde every thynge (unblocked)
by materiall figures
at suddaine view or in one houre
diversities
as might take a life to journay and pursue

       streets buildings and fieldes,
       parapet/ditch

           in number,
           forme

a bird or a humayn is it, stares at tilt of a gutter
the catt as she slips along [. . . . .]

streight ahead or downe

       spowt, pinnacle, hood mould
       from any angle

as if they were
at this time present and in doing

       pitch of a shipp
       between Paralleles
       of Climates

a new nature with maine
availe, not monstered out of a navel slit

a promise in each complexion
if the landmeater be not confined
to the upper face, as to make one perfit carpet
from a shapelesse stain

Oriall Consort

1577 20 Dec. S. Mary H[all]. Hariet, Thomas
Oxon. pleb. fil[ius]., annorum 17.

Now past the recorder
files a local lad, at the lowest fee

swears to abide, down to the black
(hatt and cloake) by statute or decree

to dwell within, hear and dispute,
imbibe the lector's spirit

think for yourself (Corano),
scan reformed maps & spheres (Hakluyt),
conjure figures through *Gaudie-dayes* (Allen)

sup and bed in Quad mare, flower of the sea
almost Ralegh's track
where a port speaks light

keep constantly
two *declaymations* every week in term
unless dispensed, by supplication
to be absent and abroad

* * * * *

Scrimary, not for chamber–deacons,
leads out to the High
by Shydierd Street or Grope Lane
so one inclined might hobnob
with Chapman—if there—and Roydon

linger at Catt-Street corner, quaff beer
in Lady Haul garden or the Swan-in-hope
between Greek and Latin
got beside pedant robes and chains,
doctors playing *yes sir forsooth*
to find if a word is rough or sublime

not far from burning pages of diagrams & angles,

a sliced pillar where *nothing to retract* is death,
a workshop with ears on the floor

You must shove and shift nimbly
under finials and crockets
(the lily hard to find)

    a great tower
    with verses pasted beneath,
    shine of rotten wood
    to roister echoes

    a little mark of the zodiac
    on the way to Quarvex
    spread to the four winds,
    water running, lead within stone
    by the Pennelesse Bench

Giddy at the stall (*stanulla*) an upstart fellow
speaks with a last saving Illuminator
as a knaves interlewde might tail a quodlibet

to believe all apparences, which we cannot
resolve, is meere simplicitie

sail under rigid lawe
and you may take your marke amisse

From narrow walls to scattered isles
at sixe or seaven shillings
pierce into chaos, grip some knowledge
flashed off risk

One theory stands with another
and who's to say if a third won't cast
all assumed to the wind

a Devil's turd for privileges and liberties—
Logic Lane is Horsemull or Jawdewyns

there may tomorrow be taste in distaste

The Ground of Artes

Mayster. Yf nombre were so vyle a thynge as thou dyddest esteme it, then nede it not to be used so moch in mens communycation. Exclude nombre and answere me to this question: Howe many yeares olde arte thou?

Scoler. Mum.

M. Howe many dayes in a weke? how many wekes in a yere? what landes hath thy father? howe many men doth he kepe? How longe is it syth you came from hym to me?

S. Mum.

M. So that yf nombre wante, you answere all by mummes: Howe many myle to London?

S. A poke full of plumbes.

M. Why, thus maye you se what rule nombre beareth, and that yf nombre be lackynge, it maketh men dumme, so that to most questions, they must answere mum.

S. Yea it were beste to learne this arte, and then a man need learne no more, yf all other come with it.

M. Nay not so. By this a man shall attayne to other sciences, which without it, he shulde never gette. All musyke standeth by nombre and proportion.

§

S. Syr, I thanke you: but I thynke I myghte the better do it, yf you dyd shewe me the workynge of it.

M. Yea but you muste prove your selfe to do some thynges without my ayd, or els you shall not be able to doe any more then you were taught: yt were rather to learne by rote (as they call it) then by reason.

S. Then wyll I caste the hole charge of one monthes commens at Oxforde, with battelynge also. This crosse of 3 lynes I pceave doth serve for those thre denominations, poundes, shyllinges, pennes: but what yf I hadde halfe pennes and farthynges?

M. You thynke you be at Oxforde styll, you brynge forthe so faste your q. and c.

§

M. Now will I propond the rule and question of a catte. There is a catte at the fote of a tre the length of 300 fote. This catte goeth upwarde eche day 17 fote, and descendeth eche nyght 12 fote. I demaunde in howe longe tyme shall she be at ye toppe.

Answere. Take up and abate the nyght of the day that is 12 of 17, and there remayneth 5, therefore the catte monteth eche day 5 fote. Devyde now 300 by 5 and thereof cometh 60 days then she shal be at the toppe.

Thys is broughte for examples sake onlye. Now learne to trye your authors sayinges: for after 57 days and nyghts the catte shal be 285 fote up the tre, and on the fiftie-eight day it will clime the remayning 15 fote.

§

S. This rule is very obscure in woordes.

M. Many thynges in the makynge, and in the use also of instrumentes, are better perceaved by a lyttle sighte. I would showe you the manner howe to make a materiall sphere before I tell you the use of it.

§

M. Now will I geve you the commodities of Geometrye, for without good exercise there is no right buildyng or sayling, as in just hewyng of stones, drawing the plotte of a countreie you shall come in or finding trew latitude and longitude. That these be wrought it is necessary to know the partes and forme of everie figure: as here the poynt or prycke, the sharpe angle, the croked platte. And so the propertys of the dye, touche lyne, threlike, likeside, likejamme &c. Let this be the meanes to husbandrye, the mariners arte: from the loppinge of trees and heaving at capstocke to the grounde it selfe and signes of heaven. To expres more exactly the Milke way, which is commonly called Watlynge streete, and what is the cause of that coulour in it. Did you ever marke the same?

S: Verily, and that often. Now touchinge the earth: this must have some forme, either cubike, thre cornered, flatte, or holow, or some suche lyke, other els a round forme, but his forme can not be cubike, nor threcornered, nother flatte, nother holow, not anye such lyke, as before is fully prooved, wherefore it muste needes be rounde.

M: Yet farther for the roundenes of the sea also you may frame arguments by the lyke forme of appearances: for where so ever you bee on the sea, you shall see halfe the skye justlye, and the farther west that you go, the later dooth the Sonne rise: and contrarye waies the farther east that you saile, the sooner in the morning will the Sonne appeare to you.

Imagine a ship swift of saile to be at the cape of Cornwall ready to goe weste. Let hir hoise saile at the sonne rising, and let the time of the year be somwhat before midsommer, or little after, when the Artificiall day from sonne rising to sonne settinge, is 16 howers longe: by this meanes at the end of 16 howers, she shall be west of the cape of Cornwall where she began her course 160 myles: and then shall the sonne be at setting to their sight that dwell at the saide cape, but the shippe shall have the Sonne above foure degrees hyghe at that instaunte, by reason that she dydde runne with the Sonne, and that the roundenes of the sea doth chaunge the horizont so many degrees in 160 myles.

S: And so I remembre when I have loked after a shyp that departed from the porte where I stoode, first I lost the sighte of the hulle as thoughe it had sonke into the sea, and yet I saw the toppe still, but at lengthe I loste the sighte of it also, as thoughe all had sonke into ye water. Which by your declaration I perceave doth folow of the roundnes of ye water.

§

M. The rule of *Algeber* is rightly called the rule of *equation*: bicause that by *equation* of nombers, it doeth dissolve doubtefull questions; and unfolde intricate ridles.

You shall imagin a name for the nomber that is to bee soughte, as you learned in the rule of false position. And with that nomber shall you procede, accordyng to the question, until you find a *Cossike* nomber, equall to that nomber, that the question expresseth, whiche you shal reduce ever more to the leaste nombers. And then divide the nomber of the lesser denomination, by the nomber of the greateste denomination, and the quotient doeth aunswere to the question. Except the greater denomination, doe bare the signe of some rooted nomber. For then must you extract the roote of that quotiente, accordyng to that signe of denomination.

S. It semeth that this rule, is all one with the rule of false position.

M. It might rather bee called, the rule of darke position, or of straunge position.

Howbeit, for easie alteration of *equations*. I will propounde a few examples, because the extraction of their rootes, maie the more aptly bee wroughte. And to avoide the tediouse repetition of these woordes : is equalle to : I will sette as I doe often in woorke use, a pair of paralleles, or Gemowe lines of one lengthe, thus: ═══════ , because noe .2. thynges, can be moare equalle.

§

S: But how I maie frame that roote I doe not see.

M: Marke this question: A gentilman, willyng to prove the cunnyng of a bragging Arithmetician, saied thus: I have in bothe my handes .8. crounes: But and if I accoumpte the somme of eche hande by it self severally and put therto the squares and the cubes of bothe, it will make in nomber 194. Now tell me (quod he) what is in eche hande: and I will give you all for your laboure.

Chap-venture

You can ryde a barrell,
you can hang from a rayle,
you can digge a tonnell

> spinne a top,
> floate on a bladder,
> playe the devill chained

> throwe huckle bones,
> runne the figure of eight,
> tag another in hud-man blinde,

> filop a toad,
> toss stones at cherrie-pit,
> chase and tutch in pryson-base

Wild is how the worlde goes at *eye-slip*
as we skip spellbound, our actes
springing from outer skie
(some quest lit like bubbles
blowne through a hoop)

> at hazard in purpose you twirl
> a whirlietrill, swag on a rope
> to shoggy-shoo, druggie draw

> this by that by
> fiddledy-diddledy
> a cowe may teach you
> to jumpe over the moone

> I'd change my Absee for Sir Bevis
> (mise and rattes and suche smal dere)
> but we are horned in steppes
> that we sho'd not turne babes again

petra, mineralis ✳ *est*
arbor, vitalis ✳ *est · vivit*
equus, sensualis ✳ *est · vivit · sentit*
homo, studiosus ✳ *est · vivit · sentit · intelligit*

So rap out nownes & pronouns,
sweare through eight parts of speach
in the Accedence, *Cato* construe
(let's take this instant by the toppe)
and in easie measure
that dyalog imbed for to morrow

where/when doo . . . an ympe in Non-age
find roome to practise sense?

I'll not be Tom-farthing but Tom-tell-truth,
not Tom-Noddy nor Tom-Tumbler
but brave Tom Piper

Learnings quick atome
in raw disportes

as ungoverned you governe,
watch fabulisticke
to get a splash
before *Euclid*
forces anie reason

Shave a peece of ash or elm, goe with the curve
toward bluff bows, hollow the hart
to make boyent, tack leade to the base,
cut a slot in the sterne for a rother-blade
and last—by hazel strippes—
add a sparre and rigge

push out in the pool or stream
to get under weigh
a frigot light as a Lark

squilge
by water-plant
leaves
in swaily weave

▷

glide
sheeney
over drinke-spill
zodiake
ruffles

little landsman
pitched
fore-ward
with fantome crew

a first gliffe
of green montaines
scattered spray

sea–twine
of jutting capes

Any plot here is big
below names rudely cutte:
a fizgig maine imbancked,
a foame circle, bobbing
twigges or strigges

O the captain is a duck
quack—quack, don't you see
at veere and tourne
that fancie jacket on his back?

Nightspell

South Hamtone

    to painim londe

a voyce

    drenched

by oare-thresh

    or shoke

in a cuppe

    of Misculyne

a lyon queld

    a lemman fonde

togedre

    lasse & more

this I thinke

    I saw

Peep into Nowhere

HARIOT/HERRIOT
(HARRIOTTS?)
THOMAS

tumbled out of
his Mother's Womb
into the lap of *Oxon* Muses,
an. 1560

but in what Parish (city or county)
no Register remains

maybe a father
Thomas
of Clyfton (tun on a cliff)
right by the Thames,
a blacksmith

at the long bend west
of Burcot

his will signed with an x (1585)

eye to hand looks true
(ring of iron)

a relation at Church[s]peen
neere Newberry (1621)

other traces covered

where? spin a vanished log

from the workshop
might come

▷

   bars
   blades
   wheels
   wedges
   hooks
   hinges
   locks

 ordered to be made
 as he

computes treasure—
3 time 10 are 30 / my face is very dirtie

  Treadable jommetry
  along the stream
  finds an angle to match
  forms gone, so
  touch wood
  & whistle

   ledges
   from the ferry
   up

  eastern slope
  exposed

a spone full to a hoggesheed
this cartoon
is a Life

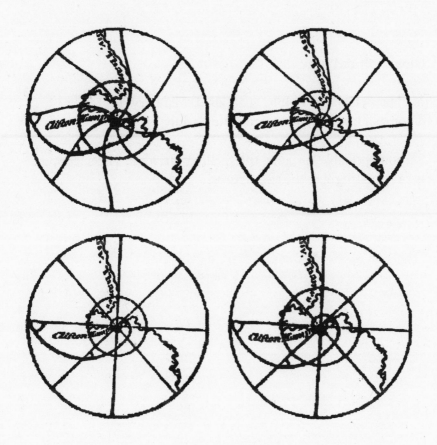

Biographical note

Joe Harriott: born 15 July, 1928; died 2 January, 1973
Thomas Har[r]iot:* born 1560; died 2 July, 1621

*Among possible variants, the spelling Hariot has been adopted here to distinguish the two figures.

BASE INFORMATION

Section 1:

Alto saxophonist Joe Harriott arrived in Britain from Jamaica in 1951. He had attended Alpha Boys School (run by the Sisters of Mercy), where other noteworthy musicians received their training. Many of his records were made at Lansdowne Studios, Notting Hill, formerly artists' studios. Harriott's most dynamic collaborators were the Jamaican bassist Coleridge Goode, St Vincent-born trumpeter Shake[speare] Keane, Phil Seamen/Bobby Orr (drums), and ex-fighter pilot Pat Smythe (piano); he also worked with the Indian musicians John Mayer (violin/direction) and Amancio D'Silva (guitar). Earlier, he had been in various Tony Kinsey groups and played with Chris Barber, for whom he guested into the 1960s. In 1958 Harriott collapsed with bronchial pneumonia, pleurisy and lung infection; this illness was treated at Pinewood Sanatorium, where he began working towards the abstract or free form jazz which he subsequently put into execution.

During the 1960s Harriott became a Rosicrucian. He supplied music for two works that deal explicitly with black experience: the stage show *Ex Africa* (1963) and the film *Ten Bob in Winter* (1964). Somewhat outside his usual field, he played on Sonny Boy Williamson II's final album, *Don't Send Me No Flowers* (1965). He also featured in poetry and jazz performances organized by Michael Garrick, whose own records brought out the gentler, mystical side of Harriott's playing. When the abbreviation 'Bakerloo' (Baker Street and Waterloo line) was officially adopted in 1906 *The Railway Magazine* condemned it as a 'gutter title'; in Harriott's time this line ran north from Baker Street via branches either side of Clifton Hill, his place of residence. He spent several months in Cornwall in 1970-71; 'Avoz travyth' is Cornish for 'above anything'. Harriott moved to Southampton, where he had jazz contacts, in 1972, but was soon diagnosed with cancer of the spine.

Intermean:

'Letter Square' is modelled on one devised by Thomas Hariot (MS 6782, f.27r), itself imitated from the Silo plaque, Pravia, Spain. John White was surveyor and artist for the 1585 expedition to Virginia (now North Carolina), sponsored by Sir Walter Ralegh. A selection of his drawings was engraved for the 1590 edition of Hariot's *Briefe and True Report of the New Found Land of Virginia*; a portfolio of original drawings, including the map 'La Virginea Pars', is held in the British Museum. White later worked with Hariot in Ireland, charting territory. 'Hurlecan' is a variant form of 'hurricane', used in Ralegh's Journal of his Second Voyage to Guiana. Certain words on the Jamestown Slate ('Bleeding Secrets') may relate to Hariot's phonetic alphabet.

Section 2:

Thomas Hariot's patrons were Sir Walter Ralegh and Henry, 9th Earl of Northumberland, both of whom fell foul of King James. The so-called 'Wizard Earl' was married to Dorothy Devereux, sister of the Earl of Essex; their elder daughter was also named Dorothy. George Percy was Northumberland's younger brother. Their cousin Thomas Percy was a principal agent in the Gunpowder Plot; his presence at Syon House on 4th November, 1605 drew suspicion upon both the Earl and Hariot. Syon is a variant spelling of 'Zion'. William Turner, herbalist and physician to Protector Somerset, met the future Queen Elizabeth at Syon, c. 1549/50. His son Peter was one of the few people granted free access to Ralegh in the Tower of London; kept on a regular retainer by Northumberland, he supplied a skeleton for research and probably treated Hariot's cancer in its early stages.

George Chapman's dedicatory poem to Hariot in *Achilles Shield* seeks aid from his 'perfect eye', which suggests both a far-seeing instrument and the intellect for penetration to truth. Also concerned with Hariot as perceiver, 'Some See, Some Doe Not' draws on Chapman's defence of his own translation procedures. Hariot's earliest moon drawings date from July, 1609, shortly before Galileo's equivalent activity. 'Trunk' is an early modern term for telescope. Hariot and Kepler corresponded between 1606 and 1609. For part of the decade 1588-98 Hariot was based at Molana Abbey on the Blackwater (Awemore) river in Ireland, no doubt at Ralegh's instigation. Ralegh, with Hariot, acquired considerable knowledge of shipbuilding technique. 'In Nomine' traces the history of his ship *Ark Rawlye*; 'odd' in this context means 'unique'.

Hariot played a key role in the 1585-86 expedition to Virginia and may also have participated in the preliminary survey of 1584. Thomas Buckner, in whose Threadneedle Street house Hariot died, was a member of the 1585-86 venture. Dasamongupeuk was a mainland village encountered by the Roanoke colonists. Manteo and Wanchese, who accompanied Hariot back to London, would have enabled him to further comprehend the Algonkian tongue. John Aubrey records the view that Hariot's alphabet 'contrived for the American language' looked 'like Devills'. It has been argued that such inter-dimensional translation contributed to some of Hariot's mathematical innovations. Peter Martyr compares the inhabitants of the New World to 'unpaynted tables', ready to receive forms drawn upon them (*Decades*, tr. Richard Eden, 1555). 'Arcticon' is the title of Hariot's lost manual on ships and navigation. As a young student, he is likely to have encountered *The Ground of Artes* and other writings by Robert Recorde. The modern name for Hariot's possible birthplace is Clifton Hampden.

In 'Trace or Traile' a misreading by Rukeyser has been preserved for imaginative effect ('Percy' for 'Pool'—indistinct at the top of a page).

————

This book was written in Northwest London, 2009-2016.

ACKNOWLEDGMENTS

For help of various kinds I am indebted to the following:

Amir Alexander, Clive Bush, Allan Chapman, Goudie Charles, Neil Chippendale, Stephen Clucas, Martin Cook, Bob Cowie, Steve Culver, Valerie Cumming, Damian Dent, Sven Dupré, Brian Durham, D'Laine Evans, Willie Garnett, Dave Gelly, Harry Gilonis, Coleridge and Gertrude Goode, Giles Goodland, Robert Goulding, Robert Hampson, Dennis Harrison, Duncan Heining, Chris Hunwick, David Jenkins, Bill Kelso, John Keyworth, Chris King, Patrick Lee, James Lyttleton, George MacLennan, Catharine MacLeod, Tony Mann, Phil Manning, Ralph Maud, Jamie May, Peter Middleton, Mafruha Mohua, Ernest Nicholson, Bobby Orr, Leon Parker, Brian Peerless, Harold and Barbara Pendleton, Jon V. Pepper, Brian Priestley, Stephen Pumfrey, David Redfern, Don Rendell, David Richards, John Rimmer, Alan Robertson, Jaime Robles, Paul Rossiter, David Sacks, Matthias Schemmel, Darrel Sheinman, Andy Shelley, Kim Sloan, Jerry Sokol, Simon Spillett, Jackie Stedall, Peter Stevens, Peter Tingey, Michael Trimble, Albert van Helden, Cathy Wagner, Spike Wells, Val Wilmer, and, especially, my partner Frances Presley.

Images from Harriot MSS, Petworth House HMC241/ix, f.7 (observations of the moon) and HMC241/vi a, f.16 (on the centre of gravity of triangles) reproduced by permission of the Earl of Egremont.

Detail from the Moses Glover plan of the manor of Isleworth-Syon reproduced by courtesy of the Duke of Northumberland (Archives of the Duke of Northumberland at Syon House, Sy: B.XIII.1b).

Photos incorporated on pages 22, 45, 58, 88, 99 are © Val Wilmer, specific designation as follows: 'Waiting to Jam: Stirling Betancourt (timbales), Bobby Stignac (bongos) with cigarette, c. 1964' [pages 22, 45]; 'Sunday at the Coleherne, Old Brompton Road, c. April 1964' [page 45]; 'Joan and Eddie at the Coleherne, Old Brompton Road, Sunday sessions, c. April 1964' [page 45]; 'Joe Harriott, National Jazz Festival, Richmond, 1963' [page 58, top right]; 'Joe Harriott with Bobby Orr (drums), Richmond Jazz Festival, 1963' [page 88]; 'Joe Harriott, Marquee Club, 1960' [page 99]. Used by permission with grateful acknowledgment.

Photo of Coleridge Goode [page 48] used by permission of the subject with grateful acknowledgment.

Some freely treated texts have their origin in material preserved in the archives of the Duke of Northumberland and Lord Egremont. The author is profoundly grateful for the opportunity to use these in an imaginative context.

'Shell and Sheave' and 'Salvage' were displayed in the Wall of Miracles project, Exeter, 2013; texts from Section 1 and Intermean featured in the Amid the Ruins series (Royal Holloway Research Centre), Daniel Blau Gallery, London.

'Proximate' is silently dedicated to Alan Halsey, in appreciation of his work on Shelley and contribution to this book.

Sections of this work have appeared in: *Archive of the Now; Beehive Poets Anthology; An Educated Desire: for Robert Sheppard at 60; Fire; First Offense; In Place of Love and Country; International Times (IT); Long Poem magazine; Make It New; News from Afar: Ezra Pound and Some Contemporary British Poetries; The Other Room anthology; Painted, spoken; Pores; Shearsman magazine; Stride magazine; Tears in the Fence; A Tony Frazer Festschrift; Veer About; Veer Vier.* Thanks are due to the editors of these publications.

The author acknowledges support from Arts Council England for one year's writing and research.

An universall Alphabet conteyninge
the [c] thirtie letters, wherby may be
expressed the lively image of mans voyce
in what language soever; first soughted
upon occasion to serve for the better to
expresse the Virginian speeche. 1585.

These names whose
power is expressed by
the first letter of the
word.

Their simple
charecters.

A table of certayne soundes which do
expresse theyr power, the which power
they are to sound generally in all places
where they are written.

- a. as (a) in all, tall, fall, call.
- o. as (o) in ore, for, core.
- as (a) in arrow, man, pan.
- as (u) in us, upon, but, cut.
- as (a) in age, ale, any, are.
- as (e) in erbe, end, the.
- as (i) in ise, ivie, pipe
- as (e) in he, she. (or ee) in thee, cele.
- } in barbarous wordes only & not to be
  } expressed but viva voce.
- r. as (o) in so, no, otes,
- as (o) in do, to, shoe.
- as (y) in yea, yes, day.
- as (w) in way, was, now, sow
- as (r) in roe.
- as (l) in lale. &c.
- as (z) in zone, zachary.
- (as the french (i) in Je, jeter.
  or as (g) in godge, judge.
- as (s) in sault, samon,
- as (sh) in she, shoe.
- as (m) in man &c.
- as (n) in not &c.
- as (ng) in king, thing, fling. (or n) in knave.
- as (v) in vine, geve
- as (th) in the, thine, these
- as (gh) in some barbarous wordes.
- as (f) in fling, feare, of
- as (th) in thing, thorne.
- as (ch) in some barbarous wordes or as
  the greeke χ.
- as (s) in hat, he, of.
- as (b) in borde, but.
- as (d) in do, drudge, good.
- as (g) in good, god, gebe, hog.
- as (p) in pan, &c
- as (t) in tooth, to, ten, hat.
- as (c) in corne or as (k) in keep &c.